MENTAL TOUGHNESS

2 Books in 1: Self-Discipline, Stoicism

RAY VADEN
MARCUS HOLT

Contents

Self-Discipline

Stoicism

SELF DISCIPLINE

Develop Daily Habits to Program
Your Mind, Build Mental Toughness,
Self-Confidence and Willpower

RAY VADEN

❀ Created with Vellum

Introduction

In *Self-Discipline: Develop Daily Habits to Program Your Mind and Build Mental Toughness, Self-Confidence, and Willpower*, Ray Vaden will show how it is possible to develop a workable plan to reach the ultimate goal of self-discipline. Self-discipline goes by many names—self-control, sense of self-worth, and self-drive. They all point to the same fact: this person is in charge of themselves and knows how to utilize their inner strengths to get what they want out of life.

Many people wonder why self-discipline is so important. They wonder why they cannot just go on as they have been going on all this time, whirling around in their merry little unorganized lives. They can—if they so choose. Self-discipline is not mandatory. It is not something that is graded and measured such as the mortgage paid and what score was achieved on the driving test. Self-discipline is a purely internal force, and whether people have it and use it or not is a purely personal decision.

However, take a moment to consider a world without personal

self-discipline. Think about what that might look like. In this world, no one has self-discipline. No one worries about getting anything finished in a timely manner. There are no priorities. There are no goals. Everyone just wanders through life happy and ignorant, choosing to ignore the fact that a better world might exist somewhere. This happy life is all well and good until the lights go out because the power was shut off because someone did not pay the power bill.

Now, imagine the same world where everyone has a sense of self-discipline. Of course, some people will be more highly developed than others—and that is okay—because everyone develops self-discipline at their own personal rate. Now, in this world, order and organization reign supreme. Bad habits are at a minimum. Good habits abound like happy little snowflakes floating every-where. People are successful. Work gets done. The power bill gets paid, so no one is eating dinner in the dark.

Maybe that was embellished a bit, but it does paint a compelling picture. Life is so much better when the people running it possess a good sense of self-discipline. Self-control and self-discipline give humans the power to do anything they want to do. People with self-discipline are more successful at work because they are able to do more work in less time and really impress their bosses. Self-employed people with good self-discipline are able to take regular days off work to enjoy life because they, too, get more work done in less time. Now, they are impressing their families. In life, people with self-discipline are generally healthier because they know what needs to be done in order to replace bad habits with good ones. They also know ways to avoid starting a bad habit in the first place. Moreover, in relationships, people with self-disci-pline usually enjoy a deeper, more rewarding companionship because they know how to take care of themselves and others and how not to fall into petty little relationship-breaking traps.

By showing us ways to develop useful daily habits, this book will teach us that the goal of self-discipline is not only reachable but desirable as well. From learning to create a plan to acknowledging reality in our lives—all the way though enjoying the rewards that come with self-discipline—every necessary step will be outlined in easy-to-follow details. Mr. Vaden's hope is that everyone will learn the joys and rewards of self-discipline and how it can be used to make every area of life more satisfactory and fulfilling.

1

The Power of Self-Discipline

S elf-discipline is exactly what it says—the ability to discipline oneself. It is the ability to know what to do in situations and the fortitude to actually do what is correct in the situation. It is a habit that is vital to daily success. Truly successful people are usually highly disciplined people.

No one is born with the ability to *truly* self-discipline. Babies only care about being taken care of and having their needs met. As children grow older, their parents are in charge of their discipline —at least in the beginning. Parents make the rules, and children follow them because small children lack the thought processes needed to make good decisions on a regular basis. Small children only see the here-and-now, the immediate gratification. They do not know and do not care that a bigger, better reward might be in store for them if they wait patiently. They lack foresight. As children grow older, they begin to see the reasoning behind their parent's rules. They begin to make choices that mirror the choices their parents have made for them in the past. They show that they are learning to discipline themselves. At this point, the parents may begin to step back a little and to loosen the reins. They may allow the child a bit more freedom in making decisions, with the understanding that the parent is available if the choice turns out to be unfavorable. In this way, the child learns in the safety of the home and with the protection of the parents to make good choices and formulate good decisions. The child learns to self-discipline.

In a perfect world, this is the way children would be raised. Unfortunately, this is the real world and not a perfect one. The problem is not that parents do not care about their children—it is that many parents do not *know* how to teach the art of self-discipline to their children. Maybe the parents are not self-disciplined, maybe the parents feel the child will learn it eventually, or maybe the parents simply do not want to let go complete control over the child. For whatever reason, most children are not taught self-discipline as a way of life and reach adulthood with no clue of how to be in charge of themselves.

However, the good news is that self-discipline can be learned. While best learned while growing up, as a part of learning to be an adult, it is possible to learn as an adult and begin to practice self-discipline skills immediately. Moreover, by learning self-discipline in adulthood, the person has a total by-in to the idea. This is a personal choice. This is something that needs to be done in order to enjoy a better life. This does not mean that learning self-discipline as an adult will be easier or faster, but at least, the adult who makes the conscious choice to become more self-disciplined has a personal stake in its success.

Self-discipline is nothing more than managing one's own personal affairs. It is a way of behaving where people automatically choose to do what should be done, as opposed to what would more preferably be done. It is studying for a test instead of going to a party. It is washing dirty laundry on a regular basis so that clean clothes are always available. It is following a budget so that future financial goals can be realized. Self-discipline is that inner voice controlling outward actions. It is using willpower to become mentally tough enough to control one's actions by oneself.

Almost anything that a person does to focus on an end goal rather than immediate satisfaction is self-discipline. The underlying problem is that it is always much easier to follow the path of impulse. Impulse is fun. Impulse is now. Impulse allows for joining the group and having a fun night on the town instead of studying and doing laundry. Impulse is the exact opposite of self-discipline.

Granted impulse is much more fun than discipline. Impulse gives the opportunity to have fun and be with friends. Impulse means staying up late and sleeping in tomorrow. Impulse means spending the extra money on the desirable frivolous toy and not saving anything this week. But impulse will not finish homework, wash clothes, follow a schedule, or save money. Self-discipline is needed for those things. Does this mean that impulse has no place in a life ruled by self-discipline? Absolutely not! Impulsive action is an almost automatic action. A cake is meant to be eaten. Self-discipline should never be so rigid that people go through life acting like little robots with no feelings and no desires. Everyone wants a cake. Having self-discipline just means eating one slice of cake and not the whole cake.

Practicing self-discipline requires great self-knowledge. Think about that for a minute. How can anything be changed if all the facts are not known? Imagine walking into a kitchen and seeing a small child and a puddle of water. The first instinct would be to believe the child spilled something. But what if someone else spilled something and then left the puddle on the floor? What if the pipe under the sink is leaking? Without knowing all the facts there is no way to come to the correct conclusion. The path to self-discipline begins with knowing, and admitting the existence of, personal weaknesses. Everyone has those things they would rather not do. People would rather not admit to being imperfect, but all are and must be prepared to admit to imperfections to be able to begin the journey to self-discipline. The next step is to be prepared to move everyday temptations out of the way. This is usually easier said than done, but it must be done to properly begin along the path toward self-discipline. Once ready to begin, make sure to set clear, realistic goal and make a plan to achieve them. Do not be afraid to set several smaller goals as opposed to one large ultimate goal. Nothing worthwhile is ever reached in one straight path. There will be roadblocks and pitfalls along the way that will necessitate reworking the plan. So it may be better to start with smaller goals that will give a sense of accomplishment that will help ease travelling this path.

Keep the plan simple. Self-discipline does not need to be complicated. The idea of self-discipline itself is actually a very simple concept. The plan to get to self-discipline should not be overly complicated. The plan to reach self-discipline should be as simple as possible while encompassing all aspects needed to reach the goal. A complicated plan may be impossible to achieve and will probably lead to defeat—and giving up is not an option on the road to self-discipline.

Self-discipline is a powerful tool to possess. Self-discipline is a positive force in life. It does not mean giving up those things that make life satisfying; but rather using innate strength and creativity to achieve desired goals. With self-discipline, life is more enjoyable, and the little cheats that help make life enjoyable when people have the self-discipline to learn to enjoy these little cheats only occasionally. Again, it is not necessary to completely give up cake; just do not eat the whole thing!

Self-disciplined people do not deprive themselves, but they use focus to stay on track when goals conflict with one another. Let us imagine that friends want to have fun tonight with a pub crawl. Let us also imagine there is a huge chemistry test tomorrow. The self-disciplined person would stay home and study chemistry, thus giving better odds to getting a good grade and not worrying about the risk of oversleeping and missing the test altogether. The bars will still be there another time.

People who have a high level of self-discipline are more satisfied with themselves and how their life is going. Self-discipline allows for a better sense of self and a higher level of self-esteem. Life is not out of control. Life has meaning beyond today. Worthwhile goals are in sight in the future—and this works in a cycle. Creating goals and making a plan to achieve them leads to a higher sense of self-control. A higher sense of self control leads to more goal setting and plan making. The cycle just keeps going around.

Self-discipline allows for more time being able to do the things that will bring satisfaction and less of the things that provide no growth or satisfaction. Self-disciplined people set a goal and work toward it. Self-disciplined people are proactive, not reactive. This means they anticipate problems and work to prevent them, rather than trying to solve a problem when it occurs. Proactive people spend time every day wondering 'what if?'. *What if the car does not start tomorrow? What if the washing machine breaks down? What if the tree in the backyard falls into the house?* Proactive people imagine scenarios and decide on a plan of action before it is needed. If the plan is never needed then at least there is a plan in place. Reactive people, on the other hand, spend a lot of time doing things that are not producing a future goal. Reactive people react when the problem occurs. They have no preset plan in place. If the car does not start one morning then they scramble to find an alternate means of transportation for the day. The proactive person might give up eating lunch out every day in favor of brown-bagging lunch then saving that money for a down payment on a house. That is self-discipline. The reactive person will suddenly start scrambling trying to dig up down payment money for a house when the monthly rent increases yet again.

While missing restaurant lunches in order to save money for that future house might seem negative at the moment, it is positive in the long run. With a bit of sacrificing a future goal is achieved. Focusing on daily choices makes living more at the moment than looking toward the future. So while planning a daily brown-bag lunch might seem like an in-the-moment choice, it is really a part of a long term goal. Deciding on a different restaurant each day is truly in the moment—and when the goal is achieved, a tremendous sense of satisfaction replaces any feelings of deprivation that may have been lingering.

Boundaries are not scary things, but rather necessary limits to achieving a future goal. Boundaries are needed to achieve the level of self-control needed to become fully self-disciplined. Setting boundaries requires knowing exactly what the future goals are and how to follow a path to achieve them. This allows the self-disciplined person to understand themselves better than most people, to be much more comfortable in their own skin than most people. This also allows the self-disciplined person to know exactly what lengths they are capable of achieving in order to reach a goal.

Moreover, becoming self-disciplined will showcase who is a friend and who is not. True friends will assist in achieving goals. True friends will not try to block the hard work needed to become self-disciplined. By making the conscious decision to become self-disciplined, the sad truth of reality means that not everyone can stay around. But the self-disciplined person has the power to create the world as they want it to be.

Self-discipline takes an extreme amount of energy to achieve. It is not just choosing to be self-disciplined—it must be constantly worked at, and that takes energy. This will require good lifestyle practices. Eat healthily, sleep regularly, exercise when possible—all these activities will energize the body and mind and make working toward the goal of self-discipline more easily attainable.

2

How to Use This Book

This book is intended to be an in-depth guide to developing self-discipline. It is not just a pleasant read to be read once and set on the coffee table to use for looks. This book is meant to be an in-depth guide toward knowing and implementing all the steps needed to achieve self-discipline.

Read through the book once, and then read through it again. The first read is merely to become familiar with what self-discipline really is. The second read should be slower and more in-depth to allow the reader time to process the tips and tricks included here and to imagine how these changes will fit into their current lifestyle. More importantly, this will allow time to begin to visualize these changes as a part of the everyday lifestyle and how the changes will fit.

Some of the ideas contained in this book will make more sense when they are actually used. Let's say that one goal is to save more money. Work out a plan to save—a personal plan. If cash is still the basis of most daily transactions, then put a dollar a day into a jar on the dresser. Take the spare pocket change and dump it in the jar every night. Many financial institutions offer ways to take money from the checking account, based on transactions, and transfer it to the savings account. A payroll deduction to a savings account might work. Whatever the method, the first most important step is to set the goal and the method that will be used to achieve the goal. Now, sit back and watch that money grow. Watch that jar on the dresser get a bit fuller every week. Watch how the amount in the savings account keeps increasing. This is how goals are achieved. It is not enough to want to save money. It is necessary to make the goal to save money as well as the plan to save money and then watch it grow.

Do not be afraid to try and fail. No one succeeds completely with the first attempt. Actually, that is a good thing. If self-discipline were that easy to achieve, then everyone would have it and possessing it would no longer be so special. Besides, trial and error is an important part of personal growth. The important thing is to begin, to try. Talking about beginning will not work. It is a good thing to spend some time considering this new journey, but the person who waits for some far off ideal moment will never begin. "Tomorrow," "someday," and "eventually" no longer have a spot in the vocabulary of the person who desires self-discipline. The time is *now*.

Use the ideas contained in this book and choose a goal. It does not—and should not—be a huge one. Start small. Smaller goals are much more manageable than large goals, and completing them is more certain. Completing a goal gives a marvelous sense of self satisfaction and helps drive one to further goal achievement. Make a plan to reach that goal. Start doing the tasks necessary to achieve that goal. Make the little sacrifices that have been identified as necessary to reach that goal. Give up the bad habits that need to go away. Embrace the new good habits that will lead to a better lifestyle and an increased ability to resist temptation. Trip and fall. Fail miserably. It will happen. However, do not give up when it does. Get up, dust off the dirt, and start over. It may be necessary to rework the path to success at this point. Maybe the failure was due in part to a faulty plan. This also happens. No plan is inherently perfect. Every plan can and should be adjusted as needed.

Keep sight of the ultimate goal. Do whatever is needed to keep that goal fresh in the mind. Draw a picture and hang it on the refrigerator. Keep a detailed journal of daily events that will lead to the achievement of the goal. Tell family and friends about the goal. The more it is out front and visible, the harder it is to ignore —and by not keeping it a secret, the chances of failure are decreased. No one wants to fail in public!

By using the ideas contained in this book and really putting effort into it, anyone can become more self-disciplined. It will not happen overnight—but with hard work and concentration, it will happen.

3

Self-Discipline Habits

S elf-discipline is a work-in-progress and a goal. The goal is to become more self-disciplined. However, being self-disciplined is not something one achieves once and considers it done. Once self-discipline is achieved, it must be considered a lifestyle —it must be nurtured daily and constantly refreshed to stay relevant and useful. Self-discipline is a habit—a good habit to have to make life more worthwhile.

Self-discipline is the backbone of a successful person. Whether a person desires personal success, professional success, or both, self-discipline will lead them to their goal. It begins with a strong ability to control oneself with strict discipline. Thoughts are under control. Emotions are under control. Behavior is under control. This does not mean that thoughts never run wild and emotions never flow to the surface. It just means that they are never allowed to control the person. One might get a little misty eyed at the birthday card with the cute kittens on it, but one would not let this feeling take over the entire day. This is self-discipline. The person controls thoughts and emotions. Self-control becomes a habit—a new personal best friend.

A burning desire to achieve these goals will not be enough to achieve these goals. Strong knowledge of personal strengths and weaknesses combined with a good understanding of how to discipline oneself is the key to being successful. Good habits make the difference between failure and success.

Successful people know that discipline is the key that unlocks the door to future goal achievement. They use discipline daily to enable themselves to be able to achieve their dreams. They know how to use a strong foundation built on strong habits to enable them to be successful. They are fully aware that self-discipline will allow them to accomplish more in less time—making them a more valuable member of the team.

But where does this discipline come from? How does one person seem so at-ease with controlling their actions and behaviors while other people fail on a daily basis? How do some people live lives of total self-control, while other people never seem to know where their shoes are, much less where they are going? The answer is habit. Behavior is mostly driven by habit. If someone can control their habits, they can have strict control over their personal habits.

Moreover, developing good habits really is as simple as knowing where the shoes are. A self-disciplined person would have a dedicated space for shoes. When the shoes are removed from the feet they are placed in this dedicated space. The self-disciplined person is never almost late to work because they cannot find their shoes. If this sounds familiar, then try this little exercise. Pick a dedicated place for the shoes. It does not matter where; the closet, tucked under the bed, next to the night stand, wherever. The dedicated spot is a personal choice. Now, every night, make a conscious effort to put the shoes in the dedicated spot every time they are removed from the feet. One day, it will be apparent that this has become a habit—a good habit to have—because now, there is no more searching for the shoes on cold, dark mornings. While this exercise may seem quite simple, it is a prime example of setting a goal, making a plan to achieve that goal, and achieving that goal.

Good habits will allow a person to create a good plan for achieving future goals. Without good habits, self-discipline will never become a reality. But how are these habits developed? Why is it so difficult to overcome bad habits?

The problem is the pathways in our brains. Whenever a habit is begun, whether it is a good habit or a bad habit, the brain creates pathways that tell the body to act a certain way when certain things happen. A cigarette smoker will want to light up a cigarette when someone else does. Seeing the cigarette, smelling the cigarette, triggers the nerve pathways in the brain of a smoker to have their own cigarette. This is why cigarette smokers who are trying to quit are often encouraged to change some of their daily habits. Smoking is often tied to other activities. Beer drinkers who smoke will smoke more when drinking. Coffee drinkers who smoke will automatically light up while pouring that first morning cup. People who smoke on long car trips may be encouraged to chew gum instead. People who drink may need to stop frequenting the local bar. Coffee drinkers will need to find something to do with their hands instead of lighting a cigarette. The nerve pathways that the bad habit created can be broken. It will take time and hard work. But then NOT smoking becomes the new good habit.

Creating good habits from bad requires effort but it can be done. Good habits take time to build and bad habits take time to break.

Start small, work hard and consider a few simple tricks that might help ease into the habit of fostering good habits.

Start by taking the time to be thankful for what is already present in life. Humans spend much more time than needed wanting bigger, better things. Once people learn to be happy with the things they already have and not waste time wanting things they do not have, they can begin to see what is really important in life and begin to make a plan to add to those things that are really meaningful.

Humans spend far too much time feeling useless emotions like guilt or anger. Negative emotions use way too much energy that is needed to focus on the good things in life. Letting go of negative emotions frees the mind, the heart, and the soul to be able to focus on the positive effects that building new habits will create. Learning how to let go of negative emotions is actually an excellent way to build self-discipline. It is a way of letting the world see the strength inside.

Daily meditation has a wonderful effect on the ability to become more self-disciplined. Meditation leads to a clear mind, a relaxed heart. It improves physical and mental health. A few minutes of meditation daily leads the body to sync up better with the mind. It is much easier to create good habits that will lead to self-discipline if the mind is relaxed and ready to receive good thoughts.

It is important to set specific goals by writing them down. Once a goal is committed to paper it becomes an active thing, something that can be seen. Goals that are kept in the mind do not have the same strength as goals that are written down. Goals in the mind can be forgotten or pushed aside. Goals written on paper are seen every time the paper is seen—and when they are written down, it is impossible to ignore them. They want attention. They want direction and planning. They want to be considered, cared for and loved. They want attention. Start small and work on them daily.

Remember to eat healthily and sleep well and regularly. The body cannot process new habits if it is undernourished. Good healthy food is crucial to giving the body enough energy to work on new and better habits. This is especially necessary when trying to break bad habits. Bad habits require extra energy to put aside. Sleep is especially important too. Most adults need between seven and nine hours of sleep every night. Play around with these numbers until the correct amount is determined, and then stick to that number. Make every attempt to go to bed at the same time each night and wake up at the same time each day. This is a good habit that will lead to self-discipline of personal habits. Of course, things happen, and sometime people fall off the schedule. But get back on it as soon as possible and do not regret one or two small slips. They happen.

Exercise is another good habit that must be settled into the daily routine. Regular exercise is important in keeping the body healthy. Usually, the word 'exercise' gives bad connotations to many people. But exercise does not need to be a negative thing. It does not mean running out to join the neighborhood gym or begin training for a marathon. Anything that gets the body moving is exercise. Go for a walk, jump rope, play with the kids in the front yard—anything, just get moving. Join a sports team. Remember how much fun baseball used to be. Rake leaves, clean out the garage, push the lawn mower around the yard. Regular movement releases stress and tensions and is another way to create a good habit.

Practice organization. Some people are naturally organized, and some people need to work very hard to be organized. If the latter group seems more familiar, do not try to become completely organized overnight. The organization will not happen but failure definitely will. Being well organized is a habit—and like any other good habit, it will take work to achieve. Begin by organizing one thing. Begin with a drawer. It is small and easy to organize. Have some boxes ready. When removing things from the drawer look at them closely and try to recall the last time they were used. If it has been more than six months then the item is not needed. Have some boxes ready while doing this. If the item is still in good condition it goes in the box to be donated. If the item is beyond usefulness then it goes into the box to go to the trash. Be firm! Do not hold onto something because it might get used. If it's a family heirloom and impossible to give up, put it in a box in the attic. When one drawer is clean, go to the next one. When all the drawers are organized move to the cabinets. As long as unnecessary items are not brought back into the house, then the house will remain clean and well-organized. Cleanliness will become a habit.

Time management is another goal that is necessary to embrace to build good habits and become self-disciplined. If there is no time management then time is the manager, and time is a very bad manager. Unmanaged time will slip away rapidly, leaving no time left in the day to do all the things that need to be done. Time management is nothing more than a plan to reach a goal of order and organization. An important part of time management is cleaning out the activities. Just like cleaning drawers of unused items, there are many unnecessary activities clogging up daily life. After the drawers and cabinets are cleaned and the house stays organized, one unneeded activity (constantly straightening the house) will be eliminated. It really is that simple.

Think of all the time that is actually wasted throughout the day engaging in unnecessary activities. How much time is wasted digging through a laundry basket looking for socks, when it would be so much quicker if the socks were in the drawer. How much time is wasted deciding what to cook for dinner when there is no set menu plan available to consult. How much time is wasted trying to find lost shoes? It all adds up.

No level of discipline will be successful without persistence. Temporary failure is not a reason to give up. Persistence is what keeps people going even through times of extreme failure. As far as progress goes, failure is an important part of life. Think of it not so much as doing something the wrong way but in finding yet another way that just did not work. In that instance, it is a learning opportunity and not a failure. This will also help lead toward greater self-discipline, by refusing to quit.

Habit and discipline go together hand-in-hand. Building a new habit is difficult in the very beginning because the body and the mind need to be taught a new way of thinking and working. But chasing good habits with persistence leads to greater self-discipline. The longer a habit is practiced, the more it becomes a part of the routine. It becomes easier. It becomes a habit, and no longer need to be practiced daily. It just naturally gets done—and once one new habit is set, it becomes much easier to add each successive one. If someone makes the decision to quit smoking, then not smoking is the new habit that will be cultivated. Once it has been persistently practiced long enough so that it is not so difficult anymore, then it is much easier to add healthy eating. After all one good habit deserves another, right? With two new good habits in place, it just makes sense to add the habit of regular exercising. This is how new and better habits are formed and how habits build upon each other to create a lifestyle of self-discipline.

Self-discipline is nothing more than practicing a series of good habits until they become ingrained in the daily routine to the point where they are a part of life. As more bad habits are replaced with good habits, then the good ones take over and lead to a more orderly and organized life. As life becomes more organized, it becomes easier to manage—and now, it has become a life of self-discipline.

4

Self-Discipline Strategies Part 1 – Creating a Plan and Accepting Reality

To be successful at developing self-discipline, one needs to make a plan. This plan will be different for everyone. No two plans will be alike. Each plan will be specific to the person who is making the plan. Everyone needs to develop a personal plan to be able to develop more self-control and, ultimately, more self-discipline.

Before creating a plan for self-discipline, it is necessary to accept life as it is now. Acceptance is the first most important step toward self-discipline. Acceptance means that life and reality as it exists now is truly accurate. Admit to what is. Acknowledge what is there. It is impossible to create change without knowing the full extent of the reality of now. Hence admit to the bad habits, the half-done items, and the failures left behind. Embrace them. Do this as kindly as possible. Do not use labels; they are self-defeating. A person is not fat; they need to lose weight. A person is not a slob; they need to get better at keeping the house clean. A person is not lazy; they need to become more organized at work using time-management strategies.

While this might seem like a simple thing to do, it is really very difficult. Anyone who regularly has problems in one area of life probably has a serious flaw in that area. Continuous problems in one area point to the reality that all problems may be rooted in that area. It is not always an easy, obvious thing to see. It is usually an inability to see the true reality and accept it for what it really is.

Many people wonder why self-discipline is so dependent on acceptance of life as it really is now. This fact has its basis in the reality that makes the current situation one that needs change. Failing to correctly see the current situation means that honesty does not exist in this reality. Failing to fully see the current situation means that it cannot be fully accepted. Fully accepting the current situation is necessary for being able to create a plan for change. In anything that needs a plan, the first step is knowledge and acceptance of the current situation. If someone wanted to lose weight, for example, it would be necessary to know exactly what the current weight was, and to be able to accept that number as fact, before being able to make a weight loss goal and to create a plan to lose that weight.

Failing to accept the current reality means that improvement in this area is not really possible. Just like in the previous example, it is vital to know the current weight before the current weight can be changed—and that number must be accepted as it is. The number the scale gives is just the beginning. If it is more than expected then acknowledge it. The reality of now must be accepted before it can be changed. Now that it has been accepted and acknowledged, a plan for weight loss can be implemented. A goal can be set and hopefully achieved.

Working to increase self-discipline works the exact same way. It is vital to know where the level of self-discipline is now. Is it high and strong, or low and weak? What goals seem to be too difficult? Are any goals currently impossible to reach? When considering daily challenges, do not leave anything out. Think of all the things that cause struggles throughout the day.

Does the house need organizing? Is weight a problem? What addictions need to be faced and conquered? Are promises regularly kept? Is bathing a part of the regular daily routine? Is a regular sleep schedule observed seven days a week? Is regular exercise a priority? Are work hours focused or haphazard? Leave nothing out. No complaint is too small or insignificant, and that is just what these are—complaints of an unhappy life. When life lacks organization it cannot hope to be truly happy. When life lacks organization it lacks self-discipline.

It is common knowledge that muscles fall into separate groups and are best trained using different exercises. Just like muscles, the areas of self-discipline are very different and require alternate types of exercise to develop discipline. The best starting point is to identify an area where discipline is seriously lacking and develop a plan to train in this area first. Start slowly at first, building up to progressively harder goals as the training progresses.

Just as when building muscle, training self-discipline with ever increasing steps works well. Just remember to start with small goals and work up to large ones. Suppose the scale gave a number that was fifty pounds over what had been expected. After accepting that number as reality, a plan is made to lose those fifty pounds. It is not reasonable to expect those fifty extra pounds to be gone in a week or even a month, but it is not unreasonable to lose two pounds in a week. This would mean a weight loss of eight pounds in a typical four-week month. In six months and two weeks, the fifty pounds will be gone. This might sound like an extremely long time, but those pounds were not put on overnight and will not be lost overnight. Also, slow and steady progress is what makes habits. Good habits make self-discipline.

If it seems to be impossible to accept life as it is now, then the only things left are denial and ignorance. If the problem is ignorance then it will be impossible to ever know exactly how much discipline is lacking in everyday life. Unfortunately what is not known can hurt. There can be no hope of improvement without knowing exactly how much work needs to be done. If improvement is attempted without knowledge of reality then any failures will be blamed on the actual thing that needed change. If the problem is denial, then there is an incorrect view of reality—and just like being unable to accept the actual number on the scale, there will never be any progress toward goal completion because there is no discernable starting point.

Following the path to self-discipline will bring numerous rewards and benefits. Goals must be intentional. No one ever lost weight, found a better job, or organized the house without a plan to reach a goal. Progress does not just happen. It must be intentional. It must be reached on purpose. There must be a conscious effort to progress toward a given goal. No one accidentally became more self-disciplined. Goals must be reached progressively. This means that once a goal is successfully reached, work on the next goal is begun. Failure to continuously challenge the status of life will not gain self-discipline.

However, it is equally bad to try to push too hard when beginning this new journey. It is impossible to transform an entire way of life in one day. It just will not happen. Deciding to correct all bad habits at once in an attempt to develop instant self-control and instant self-discipline is a recipe for disaster—and failure just breeds more failure. If the goal is impossible to reach, and it is not reached, then it is taken as a sign that this whole process is impossible. Trying to set several new goals and expecting immediate perfection is a definite recipe for failure. Use whatever tiny bit of self-discipline already exists to build upon. The more self-discipline is practiced, the easier it becomes to build more. In the beginning, everything seems like an insurmountable challenge. As self-discipline grows the challenges become easier.

Never use other people's progress as a yardstick. Everyone develops at a unique pace. This is quite normal. This is not a race. This is a new lifestyle that requires hard work and dedication. No two people will face the same challenges, and no two people will develop at the same rate. Comparing the progress of two different people will only highlight deficiencies.

Building self-discipline requires creating good habits that will create pathways in the brain that will make the mind automatically default to good activity. Think of a little baby. Babies are not born knowing how to walk. Their little leg muscles just cannot hold them up. But babies are quite determined to be mobile. They see everyone around them standing on two feet and they know that they must also stand on two feet. So they find a piece of furniture, grab on, and try to pull themselves into a standing position. On the first tries, the baby falls back to the ground because its little legs are still not strong enough to support the body. But the baby is determined. So the baby keeps pulling on the chair until one day the baby is standing on wobbly legs while everyone rejoices. The baby's brain has created a pathway in the brain to that exact spot that controls standing in the baby's legs. Now that the baby has stood, that pathway is complete. It needs only to be used over and over so that the pathway, like the legs, will become stronger in time. A new habit is formed.

Once a habit is formed it must be built upon to create another habit. This is how the path to self-discipline is laid. Think again of the baby. Now that the baby is standing, the baby must learn to walk. It is not enough for the baby to just stand there because then the baby would not grow and develop properly and would never get across the room where the toys are kept. So something in the baby's mind tells it to put one little foot out in a step. The baby does that and falls down. There is no pathway in the brain for the act of walking—not yet, anyway. The baby will build one. This is using one habit to build upon to create another.

Never fall into the trap of looking at other people in a more favorable light. The misguided thinking that all other people are so much stronger is self-defeating. This exercise has no sense behind it. The only person whose progress is important is the person making the progress. Even identical twins do not develop at exactly the same rate. If they do not, then there is no sense expecting that everyone's progress will be exactly identical. Admit that this is where the starting point is, and this is a personal path to reach a personal goal.

Once reality has been accepted, once the starting point has been acknowledged, it is time to create the plan; the plan that will lead down the path to self-discipline. Begin with a clear vision of the goal. Decide on the first thing that needs changing; set the first goal. An entire life of laziness and failure to succeed will not be corrected overnight. One goal must be achieved so that it can be used as a successful model and a building block for subsequent goals. Set the goal and formulate a plan for achieving the goal. Write it down on paper and look at it several times a day. Goals written down are more concrete than goals floating around in the mind.

Remove any temptations that will get in the way of achieving the goal. If weight loss is the ultimate goal, then clear the house of unhealthy foods. If stopping smoking is the ultimate goal, then toss the cigarettes in the trash. It may also be necessary to change parts of the daily routine. For example, if weight loss is the goal and the daily commute to work goes right past the best donut shop in town, a new way to work might be needed.

Keep the goal simple. Simple goals are easier to achieve than complicated ones. The goal 'to quit smoking' might be too difficult for someone who has smoked for decades and really depends on cigarettes in the daily routine. So a small goal would be best, to begin with. Begin by only smoking outside, never in the house. Even if it is in the middle of a blizzard or a monsoon, no smoking will be done in the house. Sometimes it just is not worth it to get up and go outside for a smoke. Then the first goal is achieved. There is no more smoking in the house. The next goal might be no more smoking in the car.

Smoking is a physical habit as well as a mental one. If quitting smoking is the goal then it will require getting past the physical cravings as well as creating a new pathway in the brain that leads to the idea of not smoking. Positive goals might include a fresher smell in the car or house, no more lingering smoke odor on the clothes. Perhaps when the urge to smoke hits it is replaced by a quick walk down the street or scrubbing the kitchen counter. This is how bad habits are replaced by good habits, and good habits build self-discipline.

Do not overlook willpower. Everyone knows that a stubborn person who just will not change their ways for anyone. That stubborn person possesses willpower. Willpower is just a nice word for stubborn. So be stubborn. Decide early what their goal will be and do not let anything get in the way of achieving that goal. Be stubborn about goal achievement. Do not take no for an answer. Do not change the goal no matter what happens. Being stubborn creates willpower that is vitally important to reach desired goals.

Create a plan, and then create a secondary plan. All good plans have a backup waiting in the wings for those awkward moments. If the ultimate goal is weight loss, then eating healthier will help achieve that goal. That is very easy to do at home where ultimate control over the menu exists. But since no one wants to be a hermit, what happens when the party invitation arrives? No happy human can resist a good party with friends and loved ones. But what about all that food? This is when the backup plan comes into effect. The plan to eat less is already in place. Now, the plan at the party might be to try one bite of everything offered and then to spend the remainder of the evening engaging in sparkling conversation with the other guests. This is the secondary plan. This will assist in keeping the original plan in place and allow the path to the goal to remain unbroken.

When setting the goal originally remember to allow for a treat when the goal is achieved. Humans work well on a system of rewards for good behavior. So chose a reward that fits the achievement of the goal. If smoking is no longer done in the house then buy some paint and refresh the walls. The house will look so much better and will smell marvelous. If the car is no longer smoked in then get it detailed; a fresh car smells amazing. If a weight loss goal is achieved, buy a new outfit, or at least one new wardrobe piece.

Moreover, accept that failure will happen occasionally. This does not mean to seek out failure. This means to accept failure when it happens—and it will. Humans are, well, human. They *will* fail. They will try hard, and they will sometimes fail. When failure happens, acknowledge its existence. Embrace the failure. Do not feel guilty or angry. These emotions, while quite normal, only succeed in stalling any future progress that can occur once the path to the goal has been restored. Learn from failure. What happened? Why did it happen? How can this be avoided in the future? Once the failure is accepted and analyzed, it can be worked past. The path to the goal is still there. Maybe it needs a bit of reworking. Maybe a slight bend in the path is necessary. No matter what happens, getting back on the path is the first step in continuing on toward the achievement of the goal—and *that* is the first step toward self-discipline.

5

Self-Discipline Strategies Part 2 – Remove Roadblocks and Practice Pain

The most basic common trait among truly successful people is self-discipline. People who have a high level of self-discipline are traditionally more successful than people who are not self-disciplined simply because they have the inner strength to set a goal and do all that is needed to achieve it.

Think of a professional athlete. No good professional athlete allows themselves to get out of shape in the off season—or even in an off-week. Muscles must be constantly worked in order to keep up a certain level of strength and function. This means that pro athletes must have the self-discipline to commit to a training schedule of regular exercise even during the off season.

Self-discipline is a powerful personality trait to possess. It allows for a stronger sense of purpose and self-esteem. Self-discipline gives a feeling of accomplishment that may be otherwise lacking. The self-disciplined person is generally more open and honest with themselves because they know what they want out of life and have a plan in mind to achieve that goal. Self-discipline is the key to personal freedom.

But just as self-discipline can be nurtured and grown, it can also be destroyed quite easily. All paths lead somewhere. Once goals are set a path is created to enable access to that goal. But that path can be obliterated by debris. Life will set up roadblocks on a clear road whenever possible. Humans will also derail themselves by seeing a clear road and inventing roadblocks. Knowing what to look for will save time and trouble during the journey. Life happens. People get sick or injured. People get new jobs. People have new babies or move to a new house. Sometimes humans are their own worst enemy. They wonder what will happen if this, or that, or the other. They put road blocks in their own clear roads.

Remember willpower? Willpower is a vital tool in building self-discipline, but willpower can be overcome. Humans are weak, and donuts taste good. When people rely solely on willpower to reach goals, failure is surely following. Instead of planning to muscle the way through with sheer stubbornness, smart goal setters realize that temptation will happen and will likely not fall in the face of willpower alone. Instead, smart goal setters make a plan for the appearance of temptation and devise a way to stop it. The temptation is a roadblock that will hinder or completely stall progress if allowed.

This goes back to the idea of the party treats. The plan to avoid temptation is to sample one piece of each goodie and then spend the remainder of the night mixing and mingling. This is a plan to avoid temptation. The buffet at the party is a roadblock on the road to successful weight loss. A secondary plan for sampling the buffet and then walking away is a way of facing temptation head on—in essence, it is putting a roadblock in temptation's path instead of the other way around.

Another common roadblock—and one that many people fall prey to—is setting up hopes that are not realistic in everyday situations. People expect that once something is decided as a lifestyle change, then it becomes fact, and the world just does not work that way. A bad habit is a habit—and like any habit, it requires work to change to a better habit. People fail because the goals set are impossible to achieve in the way they were set. They may be too large, too soon, or too hard. Remember the pathways in the brain. A new habit must make a new pathway. Let's say the goal is to lose weight. Setting a goal of losing fifty pounds by next month is an impossible goal to achieve. It is too large, the deadline is too soon, and it would be too hard if not nearly impossible to lose that much weight in a few short weeks. It is far better to break the goal down into smaller, more easily attainable goals and not risk setting up false hopes that will never come true.

Self-discipline itself will not help anyone achieve an impossible goal. Neither will sheer willpower. There is a path to the goal. It is important to follow the path—one step at a time—until the goal is reached. It is vital to be aware that impossible goals are doomed to failure and not risk setting up impossible goals in the first place.

Another common roadblock in the path to the goal is stress. When people are experiencing extreme amounts of stress, the temptation is to ignore the path to the goal in favor of taking the easy path to self-indulgence. People who are under stress usually eat poorly or not at all, neglect exercise routines, and smoke like chimneys. They often become angry for no apparent reason and may stop taking care of cleaning their houses or persons. Attention to commitments often suffers as well, particularly the commitments made to reach specific goals.

Stress affects self-control. Self-discipline will not grow and develop if self-control does not exist. During times of stress, it is quite common to forget good intentions and revert back to bad habits. When this happens self-discipline will begin to deteriorate. This can be easily prevented by acknowledging the possibility that it might happen and preparing an alternate plan. Just as an alternate plan was made to avoid temptation at the party, have an alternate plan prepared to avoid falling victim to stress. Make an alternate plan to incorporate some sort of relaxation method into daily activity. Meditating, walking, listening to music, reading, enjoying a hot bath; the list is endless. The important thing is that this is used as a stress relieving activity to combat a rise in stress and it is seen as an enjoyable activity. It is usually not a good idea to try to beat stress by cleaning out the garage. Some activities will just bring their own level of stress. Look for the relaxing activities.

Self-discipline as a long-term goal depends on long-term work. A common problem people face when attempting to build good habits to develop self-discipline is not realizing how much work each goal will need. People want instant results. Someday is too far away. People tend to try to revamp their lives all at once. They will set several goals at the same time and expect them all to be easily attainable and to last forever and ever. The real truth is that even the people who are already highly self-disciplined need to work on new goals in small steps. It is even a good idea to take small, planned breaks periodically. A weight loss goal is a good thing. But it will be more easily attainable and seem less like a punishment if regular meals or even days are built in for a bit of cheating. People are human. Only the very strongest can resist temptation forever. With adding a meal to cheat periodically in a diet plan, it becomes less of a temptation and more of a secondary plan to avoid a roadblock, much like the party plan. It will be easier to stick to the diet plan knowing a treat is coming at the end of the week.

There are other ways to build in secondary plans to allow a bit of 'cheating' to avoid falling prey to large roadblocks. Work hard at work, but take regular time off to recharge and relax. Exercise well and often, but take days off to allow the body time to recover. Study hard, but allow for the occasional night out or spent relaxing in front of the television. Humans are not machines and cannot continue running indefinitely without either taking a break or breaking down—and without taking periodic breaks, the goal suddenly becomes a thing to be despised.

Time is another massive roadblock that can prevent the goal from ever being reached by preventing the path from ever being started. This is the type of time that is referred to in "I will begin working on my goal….." Once a goal is determined, then the start time must be determined. It should be as immediate as possible. Anytime someone says that goal achievement begins next week, at the beginning of the year, when things are going better, just understand that time will never come. Tomorrow never comes. So never intend to begin a new plan tomorrow unless it is named, as in a day of the week, such as "Tomorrow, Monday morning, I will….." Giving it a specific name gives it a specific start point. Not beginning immediately is just another way of saying goals do not matter.

Always keep in mind that self-discipline comes with pain. All humans feel pain at one time or another. Pain is a part of life. But choosing to feel pain in order to develop self-discipline may not seem like a very good idea. But it, too, is a necessary part of life. Remember that self-discipline involves doing what needs to be done as opposed to what would be more fun to do—and that in itself is painful. Achieving self-discipline means making sacrifices.

Remember that discipline is often used as a synonym for punishment. In a way it is true. Building self-discipline is painful and will often feel more like self-punishment. The self-discipline to follow a healthy eating plan may feel like punishment when there are fresh donuts in the break room at work. The self-discipline to stop smoking will seem like a punishment when everyone else is lighting up. The self-discipline to exercise regularly will definitely feel like punishment during the workout! The goal is easily visualized. Following the path to the goal is the hard part.

When working on self-discipline people must act as both the student and the teacher. Humans on a quest for greater self-discipline must be prepared to teach themselves the way to follow the path to the goal that will eventually lead to self-discipline—and that is where the underlying problem begins. While people usually love sharing knowledge and usually love teaching others what they know, they are often reluctant to learn from the very lessons they teach. Think of an overweight doctor. Common sense says that the doctor should be the first one with an acute awareness of the dangers of obesity. It is even reasonable to believe that the doctor is well equipped to teach patients how to monitor their own weight and adjust down as needed. Why, then, does the doctor not follow this same advice? Because it is much easier to tell someone else what to do than to do the same thing. Think of the teacher self as the adult and the pupil self as the child. It is not uncommon to hear adults tell children "Well, I'm an adult, so I can……." Simply being a grown up is not a free rein to do whatever seems like a good idea. But that is where a lack of self-discipline comes from.

The underlying problem here is that it is very difficult to teach oneself something one lacks knowledge of or the ability to perform. People can know what to do to become more self-disciplined, but the actual process of doing it may be difficult—and when humans fail at achieving self-discipline, are they to blame?

No, it is usually some nameless outside force that caused the failure.

Think of the goal to lose weight. The outside forces that might cause a person to fail at this goal include holidays, getting morning coffee at the donut shop, snacks in the breakroom, and a marvelous sale on cookies at the grocery store. Any old excuse will do. If these outside forces did not exist then it would be easier to lose weight. But all of these things, and other excuses like them, are nothing more than the roadblocks that crop up in the path to self-discipline. They need acceptance, acknowledge-ment, and an alternate plan to avoid them. Yes, this will cause pain. It is much easier to eat the donut than to ignore it. It might also be necessary to seek morning coffee at a place that does not sell wonderful tasting food. Perhaps morning coffee could be made at home.

When discipline causes pain it merely means the person is doing something they really do not want to do—but know they must do in order to achieve a greater goal. Staying true to a goal means giving up something pleasurable. Pleasure is not something given up lightly. But to hopefully avoid the future pain of failure the current pain of sacrifice is necessary, even desirable. After all, pain can be a great motivator. The pain of giving up cookies in order to lose weight might be enough incentive to prevent future late-night cookie binges. So suffering pain now prevents greater pain later.

Discipline pain is not necessarily a physical pain but more of a commitment to a problem or issue. A commitment to lose weight will bring moments of pain. There will be a pain every time your favorite food is bypassed to allow consumption of something healthier. There will be a pain every time the scale does not show as much progress as was desired. There will be a pain, over and over, every time the goal is revisited and the realization dawns that the goal has not yet been reached.

People who are unwilling to suffer through the pain that comes with building self-discipline will later face the pain that comes from regretting the loss of a goal. Regret remains in the soul for a long time. It hangs over the heart, making life more difficult than necessary. The biggest difference between the pain brought by discipline and the pain caused by feelings of regret is that discipline pain will eventually end, while regret hangs around forever. There are ways to avoid the pain that comes with a lifetime of regret and leads to self-discipline through short-term suffering.

Find something to do that creates a great sense of passion within. Anything that creates internal passion means that it is something desirable, something wanted. It is so much easier to commit to feeling pain for a short time in order to reach a goal of something that is desired. This makes it much easier to stay on track with daily discipline. The goal must be believable and achievable.

Set priorities that are clearly defined. A goal can be interesting or it can be a commitment. It can be a noose around the neck or it can be a shining light at the end of the tunnel. Know when to commit to something and when to turn it away. Having a clearly defined plan to achieve a future goal is a constant reminder of the importance of sticking with the plan.

Once a goal has been chosen, feel free to share. Write it down on paper and tape it to the refrigerator. Tell the work buddy what is going on. Sharing the existence of a goal will often remove some of the pain associated with achieving the goal. When the path gets rough and starts climbing uphill it is wonderful if someone else knows the goal and can provide encouragement. This will help to remove a lot of the pain and replace it with encouragement and determination.

Make a mental picture of the goal. Do not spend too much time worrying about what it will take to achieve the goal. This is just a painful reminder of the pain that is waiting just around the next bend in the path. Instead, keep all focus on the goal. "I would love to eat a donut today, but I would be even happier fitting into a new swimsuit." Use what works. Even if the ultimate goal of weight loss is to be healthier, a little vanity never hurt anyone.

Choose a system of rewards and consequences. When goal setting for self-discipline, there is no outside force to put blame on if the plan fails. People choose to fall off the path, either intentionally or unintentionally. Since consequences are not pleasant, it is much better to set up a small series of rewards than to suffer future consequences that come with failure.

The pain that is naturally experienced while working toward a goal of self-discipline is a great strength builder. Self-discipline is wonderful for building muscles in the mind. Eventually, the mind will grow stronger and more resilient, and self-discipline will become much easier to maintain.

6

Self-Discipline Strategies Part 3 - Accept Mistakes and Reap Rewards

W hen working toward self-discipline, goals are made, and the path is determined. Resolutions are made and the journey begins. The way is not too difficult—progress is notice-able, and reaching the goal is becoming more of a reality every day. Then one day, it happens: a mistake. The pathway became momentarily too difficult to walk and falling off was the only option. The mighty has fallen—and now, lying beside the path and looking up at the goal that once seemed so close but is now even further away, the normal human might ask themselves, "What's next?"

People make mistakes. Things happen. Maybe the good intention of only eating one piece of cake at the birthday party was over-ridden by the fact that it was the best cake ever. Maybe the weeks of faithfully not smoking were ruined by one night at the bar. Maybe the weeks of running daily were interrupted by a major snow storm. Whatever happened, happened—and now, there is a mistake to deal with.

It is normal in life to make mistakes. The hard part is learning from the mistake. The person who can look at a mistake, accept it for what it is, and go on from there is probably someone who already has a great deal of self-discipline. The average person will look at a mistake, fall apart, and suffer regret. However, it is important to use the mistake as a learning experience in order to avoid repeating the mistake later.

There are steps anyone can take in order to recover from a mistake and get back on track. These are things anyone can do with any mistake, no matter how large or small it might be.

The first thing to do is to admit the mistake happened. Accept that people are human and flawed and mistakes will happen. Realize that it is not the end of the world, but a learning opportunity. This is often hard to do because humans do not like to admit to being less than perfect. Future progress will be delayed by failing to accept and own the mistake.

Next, realizing the difference between making a mistake and being a mistake is important. People are not mistakes. People do make mistakes. This distinction is crucial because making a mistake does not mean being worthless or meaningless. Making a mistake means being human.

Admitting to the mistake is important in another way. It is necessary to be able to understand exactly what went wrong. The why of the situation is very important. Things do not just happen, they happen for a reason. If the mistake in question involves losing sight of a goal and failing to follow the prescribed path to success, then why did this happen? What exactly caused it to happen? Was it one event or the accumulation of many small events?

Consider the goal to lose weight. The ultimate goal was set. The overall amount of weight to lose was decided. The smaller more manageable goals were decided upon. A system of periodic rewards was put into place. Then one day, a mistake was made. Was it the three pieces of birthday cake eaten at the party? Or did a disgruntled customer lead to a longer than normal workday that made the commute home later and longer in the pouring rain that led to the consumption of half a chocolate pie? Whether the mistake was caused by an isolated event or a series of events is important to know because it will assist in making a plan to avoid such mistakes in the future. If the event that caused the mistake was an isolated event, then a secondary plan should have already been in place to avoid such pitfalls. If one did not already exist, then now is the time to make one. The secondary plan can be as simple as eating something healthy before the party in order to avoid overeating, or by just deciding to exercise self-control and not eat more than one piece of cake.

If the mistake was caused by a series of events that led up to a minor catastrophe, then the secondary plan will be quite different. This plan would involve finding ways to avert disaster before one bad event piled up on top of another, then another, and so on. In the second scenario, it might have been a good idea to take a break after the disgruntled customer. Taking a moment to silently meditate, clear the mind and slow the breathing, might have prevented the series of disasters that followed and led to a binge eating event. It is important to know exactly what went wrong so it is not repeated.

Moreover, never forget there is something good in every mistake. Making a mistake allows a person to realize they are human. Making a mistake allows a new choice to be made—if needed. Perhaps the current path was not right in some way. Examine the path and decide if changes need to be made. Maybe the mistake happened because the path was not going in just the right way.

Sometimes life consists of one mistake after another. When this happens it is a definite sign that the path has too many flaws to be properly navigated for the time it will take to achieve the goal. This mistake might be the best thing ever—if used in the correct way.

So if the goals are wrong in some way, either too loose or too rigid, now is the time to restructure them. The path to the goal is never straight. It winds around obstacles, uphill, and downhill—until the goal is achieved. Perhaps this mistake happened because the goals were wrong in some way. Only the person who made the goals can determine that. Mistakes can be used as leverage to help renew a goal or change it as needed. A situation that is difficult, such as making a mistake, can help with future growth and goal setting—and the benefits that come from learning from a mistake are totally personally. They will always belong solely to the person who made the mistake.

Do not be afraid to use a mistake to its best advantage. This does not mean to constantly dwell on the mistake. Review the mistake as needed to get all possible learning from it. Then move on. Never let the mistake define the future. It was an event; do not make it a way of life. Learning from the mistake and moving on paves the way toward goal achievement. When that happens, it is time to reap the rewards of success.

Developing self-discipline often involves feeling pain for a short time in order to achieve a long term gain. This is sometimes difficult to do in a society where gratification is expected to be instant and satisfying. No matter what the goal is, finding the self-control from deep inside is often very difficult. But one of the main traits found with self-discipline is the strength to do without an instant pleasure in order to achieve a long term goal. This is especially true where the goal requires much effort.

Now that the first goals have been reached and the road to self-discipline is a familiar place, it is time to begin realizing the rewards—and the rewards of self-discipline are many.

The first reward of learning self-discipline is the fact that goals are now easier to set and to work toward. Personal priorities are more in line with the future desired goals. Having set priorities also leads to a better ability to focus on future goals. Decisions are easier to make without having to wade through bouts of confusion and uncertain ideas. Life is much more structured that it ever was before—and personal outlook on life improves drastically with every goal gained.

Developing self-control and self-discipline means that a person is well on the way to mastering control over themselves and their habits. It is easier to develop good habits to use to replace the former bad habits—not to mention all the rewards that cultivating those good habits brings—and addictions and failures are less likely to take over because personal self-control has been mastered.

Emotions can bring a person down, both in mind and in the body—but having stronger self-control means fewer feelings of guilt over mistakes that have been made because fewer mistakes are being made. This is the joy of self-control. A person with self-control is able to resist the temptations that lead people into making mistakes that bring deep feelings of guilt and regret. Having the self-control to resist the temptation that would eventually lead to negative emotions is a reward in itself.

Living a life filled with self-control automatically leads to an elevated standard of life, at least emotionally. People with self-control and self-discipline know what they are worth and are not afraid to demand more of themselves in order to achieve ever increasing goals. The idea of receiving gratification immediately is no longer a viable option. Working toward a goal becomes a way of life.

Fulfillment comes to people with high self-discipline. These people have the ability to see a goal and develop a plan to work toward it, never wavering even in the face of adversity.

The biggest roadblock standing in the way of success has now been removed. The person creating the goals is usually the person's own worst enemy. But with experience in how to create the goals, stick to them, and reap the benefits of those goals— then the person has learned to correct flaws within themselves.

The level of self-sufficiency increases enormously. People who have demonstrated the ability to set goals and achieve them are much better at taking care of themselves. They have a vision of how life should be lived, driven by the goals they have already achieved and those they wish to achieve for themselves in the future. They are also much better at defining future goals and implementing a plan to reach those goals. These people have a clear view of their ultimate potential.

Moreover, having better self-control makes relationships with others even better. People with good self-control are seen as being more reliable and trustworthy. When people learn to work toward goals and learn to keep promises with themselves they are much better at meaning and keeping those promises made to others.

Self-discipline is a great time saver. People with self-discipline have control over their daily activities. Having discipline allows people to do things when they should be done, without procrastination. This in itself will save people a lot of time and energy. There is no longer a need to panic at the last minute, worrying over what will and will not get done. This allows for a calmer and collected lifestyle.

Now that life is well on the road to one filled with self-control and self-discipline, it is time to relax a bit before beginning work on the next goal.

7

Final Thoughts on Developing Self Discipline

Self-discipline is the ability to develop self-control over ones wants and desires and use them to develop a better person. As children, self-discipline is usually driven down our throats by parents and teachers alike. There is no way to escape the constant onslaught of being told that self-discipline will be needed to achieve any kind of success in life. Unfortunately, children usually just make faces and run away laughing.

As an adult, self-discipline and self-control is much more important than it was as a child. However, if this skill was not developed as a child, then it must be developed as an adult if any level of success in life is ever to be hoped for. It is quite true what all the parents and teachers said once upon a time. Self-discipline is the truth and the way.

So now comes the time for developing self-discipline by making small goals, achieving them, and working toward larger goals. Self-discipline is finding an important reason to achieve a goal and then making a serious commitment to work hard to achieve that goal. This may require completing a task or taking part in an activity that is not necessarily fun or pleasant at the time but that will bring future gains and rewards.

Developing self-discipline and self-control makes demands on a person. It is necessary to have a serious desire to do something better and to become a better person. It creates an internal drive inside a person to be a better person—and it helps create the motivation needed to work toward the desired goal.

Self-discipline gives people the ability to control inner desires in order to strengthen the resolve needed to achieve a goal. It is a way to keep impulses in check in order to allow time to focus on the achievement of a goal. If excess energy is not being used to chase desires that are not helpful in reaching any kind of meaningful goal, then that energy can be used for something more useful. Keeping impulses in line is another way to save excess energy and put that energy to good use—because achieving the desired goal requires focus and hard work.

Developing self-control and self-discipline depends on a constant daily focus on the methods required to consistently build everyday habits that will develop into the desired goal. Given enough time and energy, the outcome will be that the ideal goal is reached. This consists of taking baby steps. It will be necessary to practice consistent everyday actions that will form the basis of the path that will eventually lead to the desired goal.

Having self-discipline is not merely doing an activity regularly. It requires regulating daily habits to systematically remove the bad ones. It involves correcting the events that lead to the practice of bad habits, and it will mean regularly changing and adapting to changing events and conditions that may mean revamping life's circumstances and the pursuit of goals.

The key to growing a sense of self-discipline lies in being proactive about losing bad habits and not starting new bad habits. People are forced to train the mind to follow a new group of rules and to create new pathways to learn to follow these rules. More focus will be needed for daily tasks to ensure they align with the practice of new good habits and the loss of old bad habits.

There is great value in growing a good sense of self-control and, with it, self-discipline. Productivity in work, school, and life will be greatly improved. Self-confidence will soar with every passing day. A new level of self-discipline allows for a better sense of self-worth. It gives a greater feeling of control and a greater sense of being able to complete the necessary tasks at work and at home. It is easier to focus on tasks for longer periods of time. With this comes an elevated level of tolerance for other people and events in life. It will seem to take much less effort to be able to get more work finished in a shorter amount of time.

Self-discipline is a hard thing to master, but it gives its own set of rewards in a greater sense of self-worth and a greater ability to accomplish tasks—and achieving the desired goal can be its own best reward.

Conclusion

Thank you for making it through to the end of *Self-Discipline: Develop Daily Habits to Program Your Mind and Build Mental Toughness, Self-Confidence, and Willpower*! Let's hope it was informative and able to provide you with all of the tools you need to achieve your goals—whatever they may be.

The next step is to begin to use the steps contained in this book to revolutionize your life. Use these ideas to learn how to set goals, eliminate bad habits, get rid of negative thoughts and emotions, and just overall build a better lifestyle. People who have a higher level of self-control and self-confidence automatically perform better in school, at work, and just in life, in general. It is your time to shine.

Thus, use this book for what it was meant for—a self-help manual for developing a greater sense of self-control and self-confidence. Gaining a better level of self-confidence will require hard work and dedication. It will mean deciding what is important in life—what can stay and what must go. It may mean giving up some events that are fun—things that were once considered a vitally important part of life. It will certainly involve making great changes and experiencing many new things in life.

Building mental toughness is not as difficult as it sounds. It merely means using the growth of good habits to retrain the pathways in the brain to eliminate bad habits—and in the world of self-discipline, the word "willpower," also known as personal stubbornness, is a good thing.

So please, use this book and the tips and trick contained inside to better your own life. Read the examples so that you will fully understand the point that is being made. Make notes if you find that helps you to better understand and remember. Read the book, and then read it again more slowly. Study it closely. The advice in this book is meant to give you a chance to make your life much more fulfilling by increasing your personal level of self-control and self-confidence.

Realize that these changes will not happen overnight. Change for the better always takes time. It is necessary to eliminate the bad habits while working to cultivate the good habits one wants to pursue. This might mean changing such habits as for where you drive, where you eat, and when and where you decide to go out for a fun evening—but know that at the end, when self-confidence is at an all-time high, that the journey was well worth it.

Finally, if you found this book useful in any way, a review on Amazon is always appreciated!

STOICISM

A Guide in Modern Society to Life Long Habits
of Self Discipline, Self-Control, and Mental Toughness

Marcus Holt

Introduction

Congratulations on downloading *Stoicism: A Guide in Modern Society* and thank you for doing so. Stoicism is one of the early philosophies that have stood the test of time because however much the world advances and changes, its principles remain relevant and applicable in the modern world. Downloading this book puts profound mysteries of Stoicism and its application in your hands.

People in every corner of the earth are continually seeking happiness in life. In fact, everything we do in life is meant to secure it, from going to school, learning how to live with others, riches and possessions, starting a family, getting a job and even having kids. Everything in life is designed to enhance joy and happiness. However, it is easy for these things to overtake a person and steer him off the right course. For this reason, many people opt for a guide or a philosophy like Stoicism to help them and keep them on the right path.

To that end, the following chapters will discuss Stoicism, providing a concise and clear definition and tracing the origins of this concept. They will also discuss Stoicism as a philosophy that people can use to prevent themselves from being swayed either by pain and disappointment or by desires. You will also get to learn the subjects, the disciplines and the virtues of Stoicism. After a thorough and comprehensive discussion of these facts, you will also determine how you can apply various Stoic principles in your daily life. This book also offers a model regimen that you can follow to ensure that you practice the virtues and values of Stoicism for a happy life.

There are plenty of books on this subject on the market, so thanks again for choosing this one! Every effort was made to ensure it is full of as much useful information as possible. Please enjoy!

1

Origins

S toicism is a long-standing philosophy with its roots in
ancient Greco/Roman times, and it is one of the major
Greek philosophies. Stoicism is a practical philosophy with an
end goal of making the practitioner of Stoicism happy through
the use of the three *topoi*, which are physics, ethics, and logic.
Stoicism includes a theory of knowledge as well as a theory of
ethics.

This chapter will discuss the origins of Stoicism, the four significant periods, and a brief overview of the major Stoic
philosophers.

Greek Philosophy

Stoicism has its roots in ancient Greek philosophies. It was one of
the major Greek philosophies and was developed from Platonic
and Socratic concepts. The originator of the philosophy was
Zeno of Citium (modern-day Cypress), who developed the
philosophy around 300 BCE.

The name "Stoic" is derived from the term Stoa Poikile, which was an open-air market in Athens. The term translates roughly to a painted porch. It was in this market that the Stoics gave lectures on their philosophy and debated other philosophers from different schools. For instance, Stoics were known to have debates and discussions with the Cynics, the Academics, and Epicureans, to name just a few. Due to these debates, various philosophers would revise their views or adopt the opinions of one of the other schools. This meant that every Greek philosophy had an impact on the other philosophies of the time. In this way, Stoicism took on various aspects of its philosophy from the influence of other Greek philosophies.

Four Time Periods

Four time periods are important to Stoicism. They are the Hellenistic Period or Early Stoa, the Middle Stoa, the Late Stoa, and the Modern Period. Each of these periods is dominated by the major figures of Stoicism and how they interacted with each other, as well as other philosophies. Stoicism has gone through several revisions since the ancient Greek philosophy was first created. Each period is important as the successive eras require the earlier ones in order to function or be fully understood correctly. Each of the periods is also important because it illustrates how Stoicism has changed since its inception in ancient Greece.

Early Stoa

The Hellenistic Period is the period when Zeno first formulated stoicism. This period is categorized by the dominant influence of Greek philosophers who discussed and debated their various philosophies in the open-air markets and other places where philosophers gathered. As stated above, the various philosophers discussed their thoughts and tenets of their specific philosophies.

Both Plato and Socrates were heavy influencers on early Stoicism. In fact, many claimed they were an offshoot of Socratic concepts, and the Stoics welcomed this comparison. In fact, Stoicism can be described as a combination of Plato, Socrates, Polemo, and Silpo. Polemo was the head of the Academy, and Silpo was a member of the Megarian school.

Plato and Socrates provide the basis for the philosophy's virtues, while Polemo and Silpo provided a spectrum for the question of are external things worth pursuit, and are they good or evil? This resulted in Zeno, and Stoicism's, unique view that external objects are neither good nor evil, but yet they are still worth pursuing. This view was a compromise between the two viewpoints that external objects are good by Polemo or Silpo's view that external objects can be either good or bad.

Middle Stoa

The next period is the Roman period or the Middle Stoa, and it is centered on the philosophy spreading to Rome and flourishing there. During the Roman Period, the Greeks sent many of their leading philosophers to Rome to educate them to bring prosperity to both societies, the Greek and the Roman. This came to mixed success with some Greek philosophers being exiled from Rome, specifically under the diaspora of Emperor Domitian, who exiled all the philosophers from Rome. The philosophers dispersed throughout the Mediterranean.

While some emperors like Nero were opposed to Stoics, and

philosophies in general, many emperors did not. These emperors allowed philosophy to flourish in Rome.

Late Stoa

The Late Stoa is dominated by Marcus Aurelius, the Roman Emperor who became a Stoic. While he was Emperor, he attempted to live a virtuous and just life. To keep himself on the right track, he wrote a daily diary where he attempted to insert virtue and seek ways to better himself and those around him. Other philosophers of the Late Stoa include Seneca and Epictetus.

Modern Stoa

Finally, there is the Modern Stoa, which covers the use of Stoic philosophy in modern times. In the twenty-first century, there is a new Stoic movement that is propelled by the ease of access to the classics available on the internet as well as a growing Stoic movement on social media.

Major Stoic Philosophers

There are several major Stoic philosophers to discuss. This portion of the chapter seeks to illuminate those figures are and why they are important to Stoicism.

Marcus Aurelius: Marcus Aurelius is the most important Stoic philosopher, and was the Emperor of the Roman Empire. Due to his position as Emperor, Marcus Aurelius promoted Stoicism throughout the Empire. Marcus Aurelius was made Emperor at the death of the Roman Emperor Antoninus, and he was elevated to the station of the most powerful man in the world. He was regarded as a god, and any wish he had was fulfilled. Marcus Aurelius was unlike other emperors because he sought virtue, justice, and wisdom. Marcus Aurelius wrote a diary called the *Meditations* where he discussed needing greater virtue and wisdom.

Seneca the Younger: Seneca the Younger is the second most important Stoic philosopher because of his influence on the young Nero, who would become Emperor. Seneca was the advisor and tutor to Nero but was killed by the Emperor when he thought that Seneca was plotting against him. Seneca became the advisor to the Emperor and was a wealthy playwright and writer.

Epictetus: Unlike Marcus Aurelius or Seneca the Younger, Epictetus was born a slave. His owner conceded to give Epictetus a liberal education. Epictetus studded with the Stoic Musonius Rufus, who became his mentor as well as his tutor. Epictetus obtained his freedom and spent 25 years teaching philosophy in Rome until Emperor Domitian came to power. Epictetus gave his lectures orally and did not write them down, but his student Arrian preserved them.

Cato the Younger: Cato the Younger was known for being Julius Caesar's primary opponent. Cato was a powerful figure in Roman politics, and he is often quoted because of this. During the fall of Rome, most people found Cato the Younger to be far more ethical than Caesar. Cato was famously called the last man standing in Rome. His ethics were never in question. In fact, during the American Revolution, Cato's ideas and writing were at the forefront of the American Founders, and they took many ideas concepts from Cato.

Zeno of Citium: Zeno of Citium is the founder of the Stoic school of philosophy. He first came to philosophy when he was shipwrecked and visiting Athens. While in Athens he discovered a book on Socrates and later the philosopher Crates. Zeno first formulated Stoicism by debating about it at the Stoa Poikile.

Cleanthes: Cleanthes was the second head of the Stoic school after Zeno of Citium.

Chrysippus of Soli: Chrysippus was a Stoic philosopher who excelled in logic, physics, ethics, and the theory of knowledge.

2

Stoic Philosophy

W hat is Stoic philosophy? Doesn't Stoic mean someone who is emotionless? These are all good questions. This chapter will attempt to explain what Stoicism Philosophy is and how it is important it is to understand it.

Clarifying the term passion is important. Passion did not have the current usage of the world. Instead, it roughly translates to anguish. Hence when the Stoics say to repress passion, it refers to negative emotions, not the positive emotions of our current understanding of passion.

The Stoics believed in examining every moment for what it is, and not allowing themselves to be swayed by their desires or their fear of pain. By avoiding applying emotions to each moment, they gained a different perspective than those who are swayed by their emotions. This led to Stoics being a very calm group of philosophers.

Without understanding the difference in terms, it is very easy to misunderstand Stoicism, which in turn lead to the incorrect view that they were emotionless. It was not that they were emotionless so much that they developed ways to examine those emotions and process them. Due to Stoicism's usefulness, those mental exercises are utilized today in Cognitive Behavioral Therapy (CBT). CBT is the primary modality for most psychiatric therapists who help people deal with traumatic events or other psychological issues.

Stoic philosophy has only a few major concepts, and they still apply to today's society. In fact, there has been a new renascence of Stoicism in today's world. Stoic logic is being studied and used in mathematics and research. As mentioned above, the mental exercises are used in CBT. Stoicism also gives us an ethical approach to the world.

What is Stoic Philosophy?

Stoic Philosophy is an ancient Greco/Roman philosophy, which was formulated in the early third century BCE. Stoicism is a practical philosophy that is designed to make the practitioner happy by practicing virtue. To achieve this end, Stoicism developed the Three Disciplines, established the four Cardinal virtues, introduced Stoic logic, and a belief in the Natural Order of things. The Stoics believed that there were three pillars, which they called the Three Disciplines. The disciplines are ethics, virtue, and physics (more on these disciplines later in this chapter in the subsequent chapters).

Stoicism is a practical philosophy. The philosophy is less concerned with large philosophical questions as it is with everyday experience. Stoicism deals with daily experience through the lens of the Three Disciplines. Stoicism is concerned more with personal ethics and evaluating the world through reason. This view is supported by logic and the natural world.

The Stoics also believed that people should be judged not on what they say but how they act.

Path to Happiness

According to Stoicism, the path to happiness rests on cultivating the virtues and growing external experiences from which the practitioner can build the virtues. Stoics believe that the only good is in virtue and that external things like craving desire or fear of pain are neither good or evil. Some Stoics went so far as think virtues are the only path to happiness. There are four cardinal virtues with the chief one being wisdom. Some Stoic philosophers even suggested that all other virtues are an aspect of wisdom itself.

Cardinal Virtues

Stoicism has four cardinal virtues, also called *aretai*. These virtues are similar to those of many Greco/Roman philosophies as they are descended from the virtues found in Plato. The four virtues are courage, wisdom, justice, and temperance. These virtues are the same as those discussed by Plato in his investigation into ethics.

The Stoics believed that only through the practice of virtue is happiness possible, and that other phenomenon is neither good or evil. These phenomena include emotions, the physical senses, thoughts, and other mental constructions, or phantasms, as they called them. The other phenomenon is seen as a foundation to build virtue upon. Because of this view that only virtue relieves passion (modern-day anguish), the Stoics made their ethical decisions based on how they can apply the situation to increase virtue.

It was Seneca who first used the virtue of justice to recognize that the practice of slavery was evil or wrong and that slaves are the equal of other men. Seneca was known for saying:

Kindly remember that he whom you call your slave sprang from the same stock, is smiled upon by the same skies, and on equal terms with yourself breathes, lives, and dies.

The Stoic virtues will be covered in greater detail in Chapter 4.

Stoic Logic

Another unique aspect of Stoicism is the logic that the Stoics developed. Stoic logic does not use Aristotle's Syllogistic but instead explored propositional logic, which is also known as propositional calculus or zeroth-order logic. The Stoics' interest in propositional logic began when Zeno of Citium, the founder of Stoicism, studied with Diodorus Cronus, who was first to formulate propositional logic. In propositional logic, the logic is based on statements or prepositions rather than being based on terms. A deductive system known as the Stoic Syllogistic was included in the logic. Essentially, propositional logic is a type of logic with a formal deductive system that introduces formulae that represent propositions, which can be formed by combining propositions using logical connectives. Essentially, Stoic logic uses propositional statements, which are either true or false and combine them into a larger logic structure called a proposition. The proposition is then judged to be either true or false.

This form of logic allowed many Stoic philosophers to make advancements in logic and mathematics. Chrysippus himself wrote over 300 books regarding logic. This encompassed negations, the theory of deduction, valid argument forms, disjunctions, modal logic, sentence analysis, speech act theory, and more.

Chrysippus was an astonishing mathematical and philosophical intellectual, and he had a drastic effect on Stoic logic.

Stoic logic isn't just the propositional logic, but it is also a theory of knowledge, which is known today as epistemology. In the Stoic view, knowledge is only obtained through the use of reason. Stoic epistemology asserted that one could determine truth from fallacy by using reason. The Stoics believed that the bodily senses constantly receive sensations. The sensations originate with an object, then pass through the senses and arrive at the mind. Within the mind, the sensations leave an impression on the imagination. This impression is called a Phantasia. The Stoics further believed that the mind could judge those impressions, which allows the Stoic to distinguish a true reality from a false one.

Stoic Physics

Stoic physics is an important aspect of philosophy. Stoic physics is a combination of natural science, theology, and metaphysics.

Because God is the universe, understanding the universe meant that you understood God to some degree. Also, because the Stoics saw that God was the reason, all things in the universe thus followed reason, and all the mysteries of the universe could be understood. Because of this, the Stoics strived to understand the natural order of the universe and to live "according to nature."

To live with nature, the Stoics employed what we now call natural science. They examined how things in nature worked and attempted to employ those observed principles of nature into their life.

The Stoics understood that there were two principles to the natural world. There was an active principle which included God and was identified as the reason. This is referred to as Logos. The second principle is the passive one. The passive principle is associated with matter or substance. Matter is divided into the classical elements of earth, air, water, and fire. Those items that are passive are destroyed and recreated with each new universe (see Stoic Cosmology below).

Stoics believed that items and everything that exists are corporal. They also explored incorporeals including time, void, and "sayables," which are used in Stoic logic.

Stoic Theology

The Stoics believed in God, but it was not a personified being, but instead, God was the consciousness behind the physical universe, and so was essentially the universe itself. They referred to this as the Universal Reason or the Eternal or Stoic Flame. The consciousness of the universe is associated with the aether. In their view, it was the Universal Reason, which is also described as the Stoic Flame. Essentially, the Stoics believed in a universal body called the Eternal Flame, which is a quasi-intelligent embodiment of the natural world. The Stoics saw everyone's soul as being a part of the Stoic Flame and believed that after death, the soul returned to the Flame. The Eternal Flame guided the universe which allowed the universe to have fate. The Stoics were very fatalistic and deterministic, believing that each person has a personal fate. The following quote by Chrysippus clarifies the subject in Cicero, De Natura Deorum, i. 39:

> The universe itself is God and the universal outpouring of its
> soul; it is this same world's guiding principle, operating in mind
> and reason, together with the common nature of things and
> the totality that embraces all existence; then the foreordained
> might and necessity of the future; then fire and the principle of

aether; then those elements whose natural state is one of flux and transition, such as water, earth, and air; then the sun, the moon, the stars; and the universal existence in which all things are contained.

Marcus Aurelius also wrote about this in his Meditations iv. 40:

Constantly regard the universe as one living being, having one substance and one soul; and observe how all things have reference to one perception, the perception of this one living being; and how all things act with one movement; and how all things are the cooperating causes of all things that exist; observe too the continuous spinning of the thread and the structure of the web.

Stoic Cosmology

Stoics believed that the universe is alive, and God is the reason (logos) behind the universe. Like Hinduism and Buddhism, Stoics view the universe as cyclical with each universe having its cycle, and at the end of the cycle, the universe would undergo conflagration only to have a new cycle with a new universe. Each universe is created and eventually ends only to become a new universe. In this view, there is no emphasis on the beginning or the ending of the universe, but instead, the emphasis is on staying in the current moment. The Stoics thought that the universe is real and has a consciousness, which they called the Stoic flame.

3

Three Disciplines

The three stoic disciplines are desire, assent, and action. The discipline of desire addresses the acceptance of fate, the discipline of assent talks about the mindfulness when making judgments, while the discipline of action has to do with love for humanity or philanthropy.

These three disciplines are designed to be a simple and clear model to guide through the Stoic way of life, which involves harmonious living, according to nature. The three disciplines are therefore the keys to living wisely while practicing philosophy.

The Discipline of Desire

The discipline of desire draws from our understanding of how the world works, that is, the physics. Physics, in this case, refers to the study and knowledge of cosmology, theology and natural philosophy. From this understanding, the discipline of desire refers to the virtue of living harmoniously with God or Zeus and with nature as a whole. It also requires one to have a philosoph-

ical attitude in life and to accept fate as the inevitable and necessary course of things.

This discipline is associated with the fundamental virtues associated with exercising self-control over irrational passions. These
virtues are endurance or having courage in the face of suffering
and fear, and temperance or self-discipline. Self-discipline is the
ability to abstain or to renounce desire for engaging in unhealthy
or false pleasures.

The goal of the desire discipline is to help people lovingly accept
their fate. This is summed up in one of the most famous passages
drawn from the Enchiridion, which urges people not to seek for
the events that would happen as they would wish, but instead,
wish that event happened as they do so that life is smooth and
serene.

Although they left their lives to fate, Stoics were no doormats. For
example, Cato of Utica, the famous Stoic hero marched what
had been left of the Republican army through the hot deserts of
Africa for the final stand against Julius Caesar who wanted to
overthrow the Republic and make himself the Rome dictator.
Although the rundown Cato lost the war, became a legend and in
Rome and the Stoics renamed him 'the invincible Cato' for his
unconquerable will. Cato used his bare hands to tear down his
guts saying that he'd rather die than submit to Caesar and his
exploitative dictatorship.

Centuries following the death of Catol, another Stoic emperor,
named Marcus Aurelius, despite living at a time when the misfortunes and plagues devastated the people and were beyond
control, gathered his weak army and led them to fight to defend
Rome from the invasion of the barbarian hordes. Despite the
obstacles, Aurelis prevailed. His victory saved Rome from utter
destruction that was coming.

In essence, the discipline of desire does not advocate for complacency and laying back. It simply encourages a person to discern the differences between what is proper and can be aimed for or desired, and what is not. According to the dichotomy of control, you should only desire the things that you can have control over because there is a certainty that they can be obtained. However, you should keep from things that are beyond your control because in obtaining them is the possibility of suffering and disappointment because of the outcome is uncertain.

The things that you can control include your actions and judgments and nothing else beyond that is under your control such as wealth, health and fame.

The Discipline of Assent

The discipline of assent advocates for the application of logic to daily living. To the Stoic, logic refers to all elements we now categorize as epistemology or psychology. In this view, the discipline of assent advocates for harmonious living, with nature, as rational beings. People live their lives based on truthfulness and reason, in both speech and thought.

Some people perceive the discipline of assent as to having a relationship with the Stoics' cardinal virtue of truthfulness or wisdom. However, assent's primary goal is to promote the continual awareness of the self, which is the faculty of the mind responsible for action and judgment, wherein the true virtues and freedoms reside.

The Stoics take the world judgment as a general term, but they are particularly interested in the ability of a person to monitor and evaluate implicit value judgments for himself. This process defines and sets the course for desires, actions, and emotions, particularly concerning the irrational vices and passions that the Stoics tried to overcome.

Through a process of continuous monitoring of judgments, the Stoics were able to identify any early signs of unhealthy or upsetting impressions and to take a step back, suppressing their assent, rather than be carried away by unhealthy or irrational passions and vice. The Stoic called this 'paying attention' to the mind's ruling faculty, to monitor both actions and judgments.

Assent in daily living refers to the ability to place judgment before reacting. The judgment provides the opportunity to sieve through the material the world presents before intervening. For example, if you hear a sudden noise, your initial reaction could be reaping out of your chair, dropping your phone and possibly crashing it under your feet in the process. All these actions are an autonomic reaction to sudden fear. However, further examination, engaging your ruling faculty, could enable you to discover that a person banging the door made the sudden loud noise. This will make your initial impression unjustified, and you need to withdraw assent from it.

The Discipline of Action

The discipline of action, also called *horme*, which means initial impulse, or action, refers to the application of ethics to daily living. Stoic ethics include a clear demarcation between what is good, bad and indifferent. It also defines the objective of life as the search for happiness and fulfillment. It also refers to the definition of key Stoic virtues, which are courage, justice, wisdom, and self-discipline.

In fact, the central doctrine of Stoicism recognizes virtue as the only true good. It is also sufficient by itself, to provide a fulfilled and good life. In the same way, Stoic ethics indicates the vices that could get in the way of virtue, in addition to some unhealthy and irrational passions like craving, fear, emotional pain, and unhealthy or false pleasures.

In essence, the discipline of action requires a person to live in harmony with all people in the community, which would require that each wish the other well so that all humanity flourishes and achieves the goal of life- happiness. However, since the wellbeing and happiness of other people are beyond your direct control, it is only possible to wish them well under the 'reserve clause' of the Stoic. This clause simply advocates for the addition of the caveat: 'God willing' or 'Fate permitting.' This is the only way the Stoic philosophical approach towards life reconciles emotional acceptance and fervent action.

Overall, Stoics do all they can in virtue, while still giving themselves to fate and the outcome of their actions in a detached manner, expecting failure or success. In addition, Stoics must act rationally, in a way that favors the external outcomes.

The discipline of action, therefore, lists three clauses that Stoics should keep in mind in all their deeds. They must ensure the following:

- That their actions favor the common welfare
- That their actions have a reserve clause
- That the actions are in agreement with the value

It is important to keep in mind the fact that Stoics were cosmopolitan, and that they had a pro-social attitude, while still putting into mind the needs of individuals.

It is also important to view the disciplined Stoic way of life as one that was driven by their cardinal virtue-justice. Justice, they defined a being fair and benevolent towards others. It is also referred to as acting in a way to serve humankind because it naturally requires extending some care or affection, the same measure that we have for our wellbeing, to the wellbeing of all humanity in a process called appropriation or widening the self-love circle to accommodate all humankind. This is the reason behind the discipline of action being associated with a love for humankind or philanthropy.

As you have seen, the three Stoic disciplines are intertwined and overlap extensively just like the three subjects they are based on (logic, physics, and ethics). In unity, the disciplines guide the Stoic to work towards consistency and harmony in their way of life, as presented by nature. By this, the Stoics were able to live life in tune with the service of the natural goal of life, which is the attainment of the good life and fulfillment. This goal is to be achieved by excelling at moral reasoning and excellence in cardinal virtues of justice, wisdom, courage, and self-discipline.

4

Virtues of Stoicism

According to Stoicism, virtue is the expertise, skill, form, and knowledge of living well in all ways. It is a critical piece of knowledge that shapes life and the personality of a person. Virtue is categorized into four cardinal virtues: courage, self-control, justice, and wisdom, which can be viewed either as single values or as interdependent traits. These four were chosen because they were found as an ideal for marking the essential qualities of a full life and because they touch on the main areas of human expertise and experience.

The virtues are:

Practical Wisdom

Practical wisdom, which is sometimes called prudence, is the knowledge of what is bad and good. It is the knowledge and understanding of what creates happiness. It is also nature with which people judge what should be done and what ought not to be done. By itself, wisdom leads to happiness.

In a way, we can view all virtues as the application of wisdom to all our actions, or simply, as moral wisdom. This is the most essential and most wide-ranging Stoic virtue because it refers to firmly clasped knowledge of what is bad, indifferent, or good in life. In other words, it is the understanding of what is most important in life following a rational evaluation of things. Stoics believe that prudence refers to a firm grasp of the nature of what is good, and understanding that wisdom or virtue itself is the only true good, then choosing to live accordingly. In this regard, prudence is close in meaning to 'philosophy,' which means 'love of wisdom.' It is the opposite of the vice ignorance.

'Prudence' is also used to refer to a person's ability to tell apart the value of different external things in a rational way. It is the ability to distinguish between 'preferred indifferent' wisely. A wise or prudent person responds or reacts to different things in accordance with their value. He is able to understand the difference between good, bad and indifferent things and determine the appropriate action to be taken in these circumstances.

Some scholar subdivided prudence into two: understanding and good counsel. This is interesting because of this subdivision associates prudence with Stoic Rhetoric, and the capacity to communicate the truth properly to others, in an honest but tactful way. The Stoics also believed that a wise man could offer good counsel to himself.

When the Stoics sectioned their curriculum into the three subjects, physics, logic and ethics, they are likely to have linked wisdom and prudence under logic and appears to fall under the discipline of assent.

Courage

Sometimes called fortitude, courage is the state of the inner being that is immovable by fear. It is the state of calm in the inside driven by correct thinking, in regard to encouraging and frightening things. It is also exercising self-restraint in the inner being about what is terrible and fearful. Stoics extend the meaning to include the ability to endure discomfort and pain. Lastly, courage is the opposite of cowardice.

Courage appears to work simultaneously with the virtue of moderation because both of them refer to the ability to have control over desires and passions; courage works against fears while moderation works to control desire. The combination of these virtues is also largely important in regards to behavior control: moderation helps us to relinquish unhealthy desires while courage helps us to overcome fear.

Paradoxically, both courage and moderation cannot exist in an environment or situation that has no desire or fear to be overcome. Stoics even believe that the perfect Safe also requires these virtues because he is prone to movements of passion like anger and others.

Temperance

Temperance used interchangeably with 'moderation,' is the exercise of restraint and control in regard to pleasures and desires. It is also the exercise of good discipline and harmony in the inner being towards pains and pleasures. Temperance is also the rational decision of the soul distinguishing between the estimable and the disreputable. Temperance also alludes to self-discipline, self-possession, and self-awareness. It could also be said to have a close relationship with mindfulness. Lastly, it is the opposite of wantonness.

This virtue is closely related to the idea of moral conscience emphasized by many Christians because it guides the thought and the decision-making processes and therefore guides a person's intentions to act on certain desires. Some researchers describe temperance simply as good discipline and decorum.

Some scholars have notably taken temperance and fortitude as two virtues that link to the subject of physics and to the discipline of desire and fear, which is also called the therapy of passion. This relationship is easier to understand when you review the exercises the Stoics associated with cosmology and physics.

As an example, the Stoics viewed events in a detached manner like a natural physician or a philosopher, and by this, the Stoics sought to achieve objective representation of them, suspending any judgments and thereby eliminating desire and fear.

Justice

Justice or morality is the attribution to each person or event according to what they deserve. It is also the state allows a person to choose what appears to be just. It is also the accord of the soul with itself, and the good self-restraint of parts of the soul with respect to each other.

Defining this virtue today is somewhat problematic because the current world has taken up a narrow and overly formal explanation of what the Stoics meant. The Stoics did not just talk about what would be allowed from a legal perspective, but also what would be considered moral when dealing with others generally. For example, the Stoics compare it to the attitude a mother has to her children or the sense of piety people have towards their gods. In the past, this attitude was broadly known to be righteousness, but modern scholars now call it morality or social virtue. The opposite of justice is unjust, which is to do wrong against another in the moral sense.

Early scholar understood justice as being composed of the subordinate virtues of fairness and kindness. Although this may not be apparent, this understanding is a much broader understanding of social virtue because it encompasses several references to benevolence, kindness, and goodwill to others as observed in the Stoic writings, particularly in 'The Meditations' by Marcus Aurelius. Marcus indeed says that justice is the most esteemed of the virtues.

From a general view, justice can also be said to be moral wisdom applied to the actions of people particularly when relating with other people as individuals and with the society as a whole. In this regard, justice is also defined as the knowledge of how to distribute proper value to each person or simply as the ability to make fair distributions in regard to the preferred indifference.

The Stoic primarily divided justice into kindness or courtesy and impartiality. They associated it with the subject of ethics and the discipline of action.

5

Value of Logic in Modern Times

L ogic is important because it creates a system of principles for a conscious mind to use when settling a problem or determining the validity of an argument. The ability of a mind to apply reason by consciously thinking and making sense of things in a logical manner is the core of a human being. However, logic is what gives form to thought processes by applying the rules and principles that allow the mind to deduce the validity of a statement.

Normally, the decision-making process involves different faculties including the brain, the sensory mechanism, sensitivity, reasoning, and the outcome. This is because we feel, think, perceive, remember and reason in an adaptive manner, both consciously and unconsciously. In daily living, when faced with problems or a situation that requires a decision, we are reminded to apply reasoning and logic to achieve the desired outcome. Hence, reason and logic are an essential component of our lives.

However, aside from this, there are other reasons for applying logic as discussed below.

The daily application of logic to life circumstances allows folks to detour rhetoric and instead, to evaluate arguments based on the soundness of the ideas presented before making an independent conclusion. If this thought process rules that the argument presented is not valid, then it is the duty of the conscious mind to decide on whether to take up the argument anyway or to decline. In this process, however, common sense is a key component because it determines what a person does despite having a clear thought process.

Common sense makes it easier to make decisions. If we depended on logic alone, we could only go over a few items on the to-do list. Common sense aids the mind in juggling the complexities of the world and provides a shortcut to making important decisions with haste. The combination of logic and common sense often produces the desired outcome.

Logic is important in daily life in the following ways:

It enables a person to think better, in a clearer way and with a greater perspective about everything. Logic has features and tech-niques that are common to all, and they are needed when making decisions in almost all areas of life. These features include aspect like reasoning and understanding concepts with somewhat some creativity. All other factors being equal, the better a person understands anything and thinks clearly and logically about it, the better of the person will be, the wiser his reasoning and the better the actions he will take.

Logic also helps to determine and identify the values and goals that are worthy of pursuing; those that are of most importance. Although a person can be pragmatic or scientific in the pursuit of his goals, it is important that the goals be right and reasonable in the first place. Logic scrutinizes every goal and idea to determine which among them is the most worthy. Being efficient at pursuing a goal that has a wrong end or promotes wrong values is not a virtue.

Logic is important in determining whether the goals and beliefs in question are idealistic. Although not much in the society can be said to be ideal, it is best if decisions are made in that direction. It is important to figure out what is ideal and to understand the reasons behind thinking that it is ideal, in order to make progress and to have a chance to reassess what is thought to be ideal particularly if unexpected social responses reveal undesirable side effects and flaws in the concept.

People depend on logic to determine the validity of an argument. In essence, logic studies reasoning or argumentation. All people depend on reason to draw inferences about things that are around us. For example, if a car cannot start, it could be that the battery is dead and we test the battery. If the battery is not dead, logic says that the problem could lie elsewhere, perhaps in the starter motor. If the problem is not with the starter motor, the mechanic will check elsewhere. For this example, the chain of reasoning is quite simple and straightforward, but in other cases, this chain can get complicated. Therefore, training the mind to tell apart good and bad arguments quickly and efficiently is quite useful and is likely to steer a person towards living life to make good decisions all the time.

Logic is an effective persuasion tool. The art of persuasion is in itself called rhetoric. Rhetoric refers to any form of persuasion that does not include blackmail, physical violence, and bribery. It could include provocative images, appeal to emotion and clever wordplay. These methods can be persuasive but will always be overrun by sound arguments. It is important for logic to be accompanied by a good argument for it to win.

Using logic, you can easily spot fallacies. The society today is marred with fallacious thinking. Advertisers, politicians, pundits and corporate spokespersons use fallacy to appeal to the majority, to reject views and suggestions needlessly, to attack straw men and to pursue red herrings. Having an awareness of common fallacies helps a person to be a more critical thinker, reader, and listener.

Logical thinking causes a person to be a clear thinker, and hence, a better citizen. Many candidates use dubious persuasion techniques like putting down another candidate by portraying an unflattering image of them, particularly in political campaigns. Although these methods are effective, they are not superior to clear argumentation. Conversely, it is the reason why we need logical thinking better than ever.

. . .

Logic also acts as the foundation for any discipline that uses arguments. In particular, it has a close association with computer science, mathematics, and philosophy. Both modern symbolic logic and Aristotelian logic have been used extensively in bodies of knowledge that promote major intellectual achievements.

Career training and any progression thereafter are wholly reliant on logic and reasoning. Careers in finance, law, chemistry, archeology, administration, engineering, history, and other disciplines consider logic an essential requirement. It has been the force behind innovation, inventions, and research. It is the reason the world is able to broaden the range of things it knows and understands, makes predictions and acquires a sense of direction. For individuals, logic is also the key to self-renewal, self-discovery and the expansion of consciousness.

Logic allows a person to see through emotions. Many people who are said to be emotional often allow emotions to get in the way of making a solid decision. However, logic sifts through the emotions and other outliers to come up with the best solution. For example, persons earning low wages are able to survive and educate their children based on logic. They eliminate the unnecessary and prioritize on essential commodities. Logic is also the tool that people use to fit a number of activities into one schedule. It prevents dwelling on one issue as emotion would have you do, causes a person to compromise, and in the end do all that the person was scheduled to do.

Logic serves as the basis for building, structuring and presenting proofs. Some truths may be difficult to understand, or that the proof may not be available. For example, in a court case, the court may not be able to recreate the circumstances under which some event happened. However, using logic, the lawyers and the judge are able to deduce what happened based on the available facts, evidence, and confessions from witnesses. Using logic, the court is able to distinguish between true testimony and false evidence and accusations.

Logic offers a way to improve a person's critical thinking skills because the person is able to study the problem and implement different strategies to come up with a solution. This process involves both deductive and inductive reasoning. Deductive reasoning is the process that one takes to come up with a solution beginning from stating the facts and definitions, down to the part where a solution is derived. Inductive reasoning, on the other hand, is the process in which a conclusion is made merely based on observations.

Overall, logic is about being rational, consistent and non-contradictory. It has nothing to do with personal values and beliefs; it is only a means to a result, aimed at helping us think and apply critical thinking skills. In reality, logic may cause a person to change his beliefs and opinions after rationally thinking through a particular standpoint.

6

Improving Your Life

B ack in the third century when Stoicism developed in Rome and ancient Greece, people spent much of their time thinking and coming up with strategies, they would practice to enable them to live a good life. Many people strived to live happily and righteously, possessing a good soul. This was not just a conversation in dinner parties; the issue was even talked about in the streets. This constant probing made Stoicism quite popular primarily because it answered many of life's big questions. It dealt with the problems that people struggled with at the time, fear, stress and anxiety, in a simple yet elegant way.

Stoics believed that living a good life, and enjoying the tranquility of the mind required a person to be virtuous and of excellent character. Looking at this belief carefully and practically, isn't it true that a good character is essential for a person to live well and happily? Don't we greatly admire people who keep calm and remain kind in stressful situations? Doesn't a good character go before wealth and riches? Doesn't it help to remain your best self whatever comes your way?

Indeed, the Stoic way of life was popular for a reason-the system worked. Although Stoic principles were developed so long ago, the truth is that the strategies work. Modern people can still find value and improve their lives following the Stoic principles. These are not ideas to be kept in mind, but rather, they are to be practiced daily.

They include:

Every good or bad intention in a man lies in his will -Epictetus

Once again, the Stoics' primary concern was to practice virtue. This, they considered being more important than health or wealth. Attaining an excellent character was equated to acquiring the highest good in the society. Stoics also believed that as long as they exercised virtuous thinking and behavior by caring only for the things that are under their control, they need not concern themselves with external events beyond their control.

Living under this principle in the modern world, you ought to understand that you are in charge of what you feel inside and what you contribute to the world around you. You are not responsible for what others say, think or do. Therefore, even though people are rude or racist to you, or you come across a streak of bad luck, nothing should deter you from being and acting your best. You are in full control of how you respond to what is thrown at you, and as long as you are virtuous in your ways, you can relax in the knowledge and belief that you are living a good life.

It is impossible to have everything you want, but you have the ability and power of not wanting what you cannot have. Therefore, only spend your energy putting what you have to good use. —Seneca

When you adopt the stoic way of life, you will not have to give up material goods. In fact, material goods are embraced and encouraged, but only to the extent that they enhance a person's ability to live a life of virtue. Stoics were particularly aware of the danger of consumerism and the emotions or actions it triggers.

The Stoic lifestyle does not require you to give up your dream of owning a sports car or a jet in the future; it only requires you to be grateful for what you have more than what is yet to come. Most people spend significant energy and time trying to come up with ways they can own bigger homes or cooler cars despite having excellent health and owning more than others do. However, Stoicism advises people not to worry about what they do not have and instead, to be constantly aware of what they have and develop gratitude for it.

One of the famous Stoics, Seneca, was known to have days of poverty where he ate no food and wore unfashionable clothes. This exercise was meant to convince him and others that a person does not need luxuries to enjoy a good life. In fact, a person with a great character was perceived to be living a good life even without riches.

The society today values possession than values. One of the problems that have crippled governments across the world is corruption, as government officials, civil servants, and others steal and embezzle public funds for personal gain. Most people see leadership positions as avenues to enrich themselves with what is meant for personal gain. The problem is not only at the top, but the grassroots are also marred with conmen, unscrupulous businesspersons, thieves, online frauds and others that are trying to make some money off of others. The religious sector is also affected by the rise of leaders who are only out to mint some money at the expense of their followers. The end result is a world that is overcome by greed and the need to accumulate more than individuals need. People who are virtuous and just are considered unwise and despised in society.

However, embracing the Stoic way of life calls for a change of the current mindset so that people begin to value integrity and the pursuit of good living other than the accumulation of possessions. It also means that people begin to notice and enjoy what they have other than focusing on what is missing. This, however, does not advocate for complacency where people no longer pursue a higher life, it only means that the pursuit of material items becomes secondary and no longer the driver of habits and intentions in people.

Do not argue and debate on what a good man ought to be like, instead, be one. –Marcus Aurelius

It was believed that a true Stoic is one who gets up and practices the virtues and the way of life he advocates for. The Stoics considered talk cheap and upheld action. Instead of only having it in writing, the stoics wanted the values of a good man to be displayed by action. Therefore, each man who desired to be called 'good' in society had to earn it by his character.

In the same way, we must live as the good people we want to be seen as. It is of no benefit to having a constitution, religious values and other good things we uphold with our mouths and not our characters. For example, people who believe in the rights of all the citizens should not practice racism, sexism and other forms of discrimination. If indeed a person upholds a constitution that calls for the equality of all persons, he should go by what the constitution says and respect people of all color, gender, religion, age, body size and other kinds of differences.

Marcus Aurelius' quote also shows the value that the Stoics

placed on moral integrity and righteous living. They considered those who lived uprightly on a daily basis to be good. If a person considers himself kind, then he should commit acts of kindness every day. A person seeking to become a counselor should offer counseling and advice to people on a daily basis. Therefore, your words must bring your values to life through daily action. Therefore, every day, pursue kindness, love, honesty, and creativity.

It is unfortunate, not lucky, to have never had misfortune in life because when you live without an opponent in life, you will not know what you are capable of. –Seneca

The Stoics view misfortune differently than many people. They anticipate misfortunes and use them as opportunities to perfect their virtues and build their inner agility. This does not mean that they are happy when troubles come against them, they only choose not to lament them pointlessly, and instead seek to benefit from them as much as possible.

In the event of an accident or incident that incapacitates temporarily, a Stoic would make an effort to guide his thoughts away from self-pity, rumination, and other useless thoughts. Instead, a Stoic will seek to be productive in his immobility. For example, he will use the event as a focal point for cultivating more patience and creativity. The Stoic will not allow the unfortunate event to ruin to get in the way of his peace. Instead, he will work to ensure that the event contributes to the building of his character as much as possible.

In the embodiment of this virtue, the society today should also seek benefits from adversities. Expect that occasionally, something adverse and catastrophic will happen to you, and this event is likely to dampen your spirits and mood. However, the right way to respond is to use the adverse event as a stepping-stone to greatness. Do not allow the event to take away your peace and joy, but use it as a learning opportunity. The only thing you have to avoid is feeling sorry for yourself because it is pointless and does not yield any solution.

What happens externally is not the issue, the issue is how you assess and interpret them, but this assessment and interpretation can be changed. – Marcus Aurelius

In all situations, your mind and your thoughts determine how you experience reality. It is possible for two people to go through the same hardship but have completely different assessments of the same events, and have a significant difference in the behaviors and emotions they portray. For example, one may be miserable for losing a job while another will feel liberated and welcome the opportunity to be helpful elsewhere. In this case, the same situation has produced different thoughts and different outcomes.

Stoics believed that things had to take their natural course and so if something bad was meant to happen, it had to happen. With this knowledge, these people did not see the need for sitting around and playing these events in their minds especially when this would only intensify their suffering. Instead, the Stoics would teach on the need to change your thought pattern to maintain the serenity of the mind.

Borrowing from the Stoics, it is best to refrain from worry and anxiety about what is to happen, especially when you cannot change the outcome of events. Instead of sitting around biting your nails, find something else to do. When you are busy working on one thing, it is difficult to keep worrying about another. Distracting yourself keeps you at peace. When the results arrive, you will deal with them as required, but for now, maintain your calm.

It is also important to remember that your thought process will influence your behavioral and emotional reaction. If you are a little more optimistic, you are likely to behave better and feel better in the situation. If on the other hand are led by worry and anxiety, you are likely to feel miserable and to engage in activities that could have you regret later on. Try to adopt this life-changing strategy, and you will find that you are even able to think logically in the heat of the situation.

Maya Angelou sums this principle by stating that if you are displeased about something, you should do something to change it. However, if you cannot change, she recommends changing your attitude instead.

Make sure to keep death and exile in your vision every day, in addition to everything else that seems terrible because by doing this, you will not have a base thought or develop excessive desire. —Epictetus

Make ready your mind as though you are at the end of your life, postponing nothing. Balance the books of your life each day because a person who makes the final touches of his life has not run out of time. –Seneca

The statements above depict important philosophical tradition practices by the Stoics, up unto the Existentialists. The concept, Memento Mori, reminds people that they will die. This may be saddening, but the Stoics believed that thinking about death could rouse some gratitude and more deeds of virtue.

When a person understands that his life is finite, they get a realization of the important things in life. The idea behind this is to get people to live today like they never will again. It is also meant to help them keep off stress particularly that pertaining small things in the understanding that the little things could be robbing them of the joy of the moment.

In the same way, if you want to live a fulfilling life, live in the moment, capturing all the life and the energy of the moment. It is also the secret to avoiding stress-related diseases like high blood pressure and stomach ulcers. In addition, when you remain calm, you are able to view a situation from different angles, which makes you more objective in your decision-making and as you weigh out issues.

Lastly, when you know that life could end at any moment, you are less likely to carry too much baggage to heart. If someone does something against you, you are less likely to care about it knowing that he will not have a chance to hurt you again. This attitude breeds forgiveness, which is a critical requirement for leading a physically and emotionally healthy life.

> *The primary responsibility in life is that of identifying and separating matters so that you are able to see for yourself clearly the factors over which you have control and the external factors that are not in your control. Knowing this, seek to differentiate the good and the evil only from what you can control within yourself, and not from uncontrollable external factors.*
> *—Epictetus*

This statement reiterates the fact that Stoics acknowledged that they lacked control over the majority of what happens in life. Therefore, they count worrying about uncontrollable things as unproductive for a person seeking to enjoy the peace and to have a good life. Stoics insist that what should matter in life is what you have control over.

On a daily basis, a Stoic would remind you to actively sort through what you can and what you cannot control. After keeping off the uncontrollable events, now work on creating virtuous thoughts and deeds, which are always under the control of your mind.

Many people waste so much time and energy pondering over things that happened many years ago and cannot be changed. Others desire things they cannot have as a way to prove to others that they have succeeded. This process of worrying and trying to keep appearances only exasperates the people and leaves them emotionally and physically drained. Therefore, ensure that you remain conscious of what is in your mind, and only think of things that you can affect.

7

Applications of the Three
Disciplines

A t the start of the third century BC, the Stoics came up with a plan and a way of life that would emphasize happiness. They taught that everyone has the ability to produce their happiness because it does not depend on the actions or the opinions of others. To them, philosophy was not just a bunch of ideas but a way of life that continues to be relevant to this day.

Many of the Stoic concepts are applicable to the modern age, including the three Stoic disciplines: action, desire, and assent. The discipline of desire has to do with exercising self-control over irrational passions, the discipline of action has to do with the application of ethics to daily living while the discipline of assent advocates for the application of logic to daily living. These concepts are applicable in our world today.

Use the Interconnectedness for Good

One of the ways Stoicism applies is in the use of technology where it reminds us that we are interconnected like one family.

Although stoicism advocates for an inward look for one to check one's thoughts and character, this is not to mean that stoicism is an egoistic philosophy promoting self-centeredness. However, part of human nature is the desire to benefit from one another. Seneca says that nothing excites the mind as much as loyal and fine friendship does. Hierocles described the relationship between human beings as concentric circles, similar to those of an onion beginning with the self, the family, and others according to the value a person has placed on each group. This interconnectedness was already a 'thing' before the interconnectedness the internet has graced us with today.

Today, in our phones and at our fingertips are the tools the world needs to bring to life this shared kinship. Courtesy of the internet, cultures around the world is now able to interact and overlap. We maintain connections politically, economically and socially. People from New York, London, Riyadh, and Nairobi will share the same stories and even discuss events like episodes from popular TV series like Game of Thrones and Blindspot. The more interconnected we become, the more our fates coincide so that we now rise and fall together.

Despite the interconnection and the overlapping interests, the world remains ethnically isolated. The same biases, images and advertisements, and promises continue to flock our screens with a guarantee that whatever is placed on the internet will spread fast. Many times, the negative strains like hostility and anger are the ones that will spread quite easily. The result is that this interconnectedness tears the people apart makes them less trusting and angrier.

Nevertheless, if we all follow the Stoic way of life and strive to achieve personal goodness, living according to the best of our characters, we will not help but promote the good in the society.

People will be gentler and more empathetic, friendly and courteous, humane, discrete and merciful, among other honorable qualities. These qualities will bind us all together. They will successful transform large variant communities into groups of friends and confidants.

Avoid Setting Very High Expectations

The stoic disciplines will also have you living with virtue and lowering your expectations to avoid getting hurt after not getting what you expected. This is true because although technology connects us and brings many good things on the world closer, it sometimes fails to deliver on its promises. Technology is able to connect to a person's basest, deepest and cheapest desires and therefore, when all that is taken away, it leaves the people feeling empty. With this feeling of lack and emptiness, as we try to make sense of what is happening, it is easy to be allured by the images and the ideas that are packaged as the alternative sources of happiness. However, many times, these allures are only meant to promote or sell ideas and commodities, and will not be a substitute for joy and do not contribute to the wellbeing of a person.

Be Cautious About the Desires You Develop

It is also proven that insatiable desire can destroy a gentle heart. Stoics agree with Buddhists that insatiable desire only causes unhappiness. The modern equivalent of this desire is set very high expectations and having low resilience. If the resilience does not rise to the level of the expectations, you can become desperate. However, to be happy, a person must have the resilience that goes beyond what they expect.

While there are many paths to achieving happiness, one popular principle is that of being a minimalist. If you live continually trying to reach the high expectations, it is likely that you will not be able to appreciate the less you have. However, when you have learned to appreciate and to live by the less, you will be less concerned about the expectations. You will begin to flourish. Constantly seeking more creates a sense of lack that keeps you from enjoying the present. Wealth becomes more fulfilling and a greater luxury when you know how to live without it.

Some people say that the way to be ambitious is to create a long list of needs so that they have something to work on continuously. However, what this does is create insatiability and a constant struggle inwardly. This is the reason millionaires, billionaires and other wealthy people you know are said to be most troubled. They create a list of things they must achieve to get to the top, for fame.

Many will acquire a yacht after another, cars, planes and jets, all in the name of creating a name. Many of them become angry, disappointed and even depressed when someone else is said to be richer than them. That said, there are also many people who are wealthy and happy. It all depends on what is in the individual's heart. An unquenchable desire will only burn through a faint heart. However, being courageous and living life on your terms will pick you back up.

Set Internal Goals before the External Ones

While no one would need help setting external goals, only disciplined people know how to set internal goals. However, setting internal goals is easy. It requires an inner focus when seeking solutions to resolve problems you could have within yourself. For example, instead of aspiring to have a car that you cannot afford to keep yourself from getting late for work, focus on developing the discipline of waking up early and being on time. Rather than overworking yourself to earn more money, focus on developing self-regulation so that you become a better manager of the little you have now. Life is a tempest sometimes, and only self-control will keep you from getting carried away. When you have figured out the internal, external accomplishments will start to increase. A disciplined person is likely to accomplish much in only a short time, even when it involves doing things you would rather not do.

Develop Some Controls and Discipline

How do you increase your discipline? The fact is that all of us have some measure of discipline, but some engage in exercises to increase it, while the rest do not. However, discipline is key towards reaching your goals; whether you want to start a business, build a new house or lose some weight, you need to behave differently from what your emotions are having you do. There are days when it is difficult to maintain a specific mindset when you will feel like it is not worth it but if in the midst of that you remain disciplined, you will succeed at exercising self-control.

The Stoics believe that if you lack a philosophy in life, you are likely to result in automatic responses to seek pleasure and to acquire instant gratification. Many times, emotions get in the way of exercising free will and make us slaves to the happenings of the day. Sometimes, we think of disciplined people as robotic while in an actual sense, not being able to control your emotions and behavior is what makes you robotic. However, what makes a person human is the ability to reason and to come up with better ways to resolve a problem. Delaying gratification is the way to developing long-term commitment. Although giving in to an urge and a temptation will grant you temporary satisfaction, true happiness comes from growing as a person and reaching your goals the right way.

Be Mindful

One of the key aspects of Stoicism is mindfulness. It allows you to recognize and tell apart the things that you have control over and those that you have none. If you are desperate and frustrated because of the events that are beyond your control, you will be fostering negativity and wasting energy. This is best illustrated by the story of Buddha, with Buddha as the enemy and Mara as the antagonist.

In the story, Mara learned about the powers of Buddha and sought to destroy him; Mara put together a large, powerful army. He instructed the soldiers to throw burning rocks at Buddha, but when the burning rocks got near Buddha, they transformed into flowers and fell to the ground. Desperate, Mara asked his army to throw arrows at Buddha, but the arrows also became flowers when they got close to Buddha. As you can see, there is not a thing Mara could do against Buddha because Buddha had learned how to shelter his peace and happiness from outside influences.

The burning rocks and the arrows are parallel to the negative thoughts and external circumstances that could deter your joy. Since you cannot control what is coming at you, you can only control the attitude you have towards what is coming. Once you have fully understood and realized it, your mind shall become impenetrable because as long as you have power over your reactions and attitudes, you will hardly be influenced by others and what they do.

Therefore, whenever passions flare up, despite the hopes and the expectations we have, the basic question is, "To which direction do you expect your life to take?" If you live a virtuous life, it is likely that people will 'like,' 'follow' and 'retweet' your sentiments, and other times, the people may not even notice or validate what you do. Either way, live by virtue, whether people realize it or not.

What Matters At the End of Life

The only things that matter at the end of life are integrity and character. Therefore, do not lower your standards because of the circumstances, the fear or the desire. Do not be tied down by the standards and the expectations of others because once you align yourself with the best and the highest aspects of nature, you will be able to increase your independence, moderate anger, restrain ambition, practice frugality and regard others without prejudice. It is through virtuous living that you will find joy and true happiness in life.

8

Relevance of the Virtues

In the Stoic way of life, virtue is the expertise, form, skill or knowledge of how to live well in all spheres of life. It is a form of knowledge that defines a person's personality and life. It is analyzed in the form of four values: wisdom, moderation, self-control, and courage as discussed earlier. So, why the four qualities?

The four qualities were chosen because they rightfully cover and map all major areas of human expertise and experience, and when taken together, they constitute the qualities you need to lead a full life. Wisdom gives a person the understanding of how to feel and act correctly while self-control gives a person the knowledge of how to feel or act appropriately in situations that arouse emotions like lust, desire, appetite, and other similar feelings.

Courage gives knowledge of how to feel and act correctly in danger and when facing fear such as that of death while justice makes a person know how to feel and act properly when relating with others from an individual, familial and community level. All these virtues teach people how to treat others with generosity, compassion, with friendship and showing affection.

Each virtue affects how you relate to yourself and with others, although some like justice have an inward focus in comparison to others. However, all these virtues work for the benefit of ourselves and of others because they affect how you think of yourself, the blame you place on yourself, the expectations you have on what you should accomplish, and those that you have of others. This is fundamental in Stoicism.

The relevance of these virtues is based on the following:

- **The Virtues are Attainable**

The Stoic virtues are of importance because they show that the Stoics firmly believed that all human beings are capable of attaining these virtues. Developing wisdom, justice, self-control, and courage do not require the holder to have any special inborn qualities, a special intellectual background or a special social background. The Stoics believed that all human beings already have the 'starting points' for these values.

This belief is based on the assumption that all human beings have an innate capacity to develop ethical notions such as the ability to know what is good, to give it context and content in any social environment they find themselves. However, more importantly, the Stoics emphasize the importance of growth in ethical understanding because no one gets to possess these virtues just like that; they develop in a long process and keep growing throughout a person's lifetime. It is impossible to be whole and complete, needing no further guidance and instruction.

Development of the virtues is measured in terms of making improvement in understanding and making improvements in the development of social and interpersonal relationships until you are able to perceive all human beings as sisters and brothers pursuing ethics as well. Therefore, as humans, we are all on the path of virtue, and we seek to make continual progress in life.

- **Virtues are Necessary for the Wholesome Development of a Person**

Perceiving the virtues as forms of knowledge is misconstrued because this makes them sound purely cognitive and rational, which is a very narrow perspective. However, from the Stoic understanding, the four virtues were meant to aid in the development of a person as a whole, including the desires and emotions. This is in line with Stoic thinking, which states that we function as unified, holistic agents and that our reasoning and beliefs shape the way we desire, and feel.

- **The Development of Virtue Causes a Radical Change in a Person's Emotional Life**

Stoicism leads to maturity and growth in the way people deal with emotions so that they cease to experience bad or misguided emotions like fear, appetite, anger, and craving, and they only feel good emotions. Misguided emotions are based on what people regard as a false ethical judgment that causes intense, disturbing effects on both the mind and the body physiology. Good emotions, on the other hand, are developed from sound ethical judgments derived from the virtues, and they lead to calmer pleasant effects on the psychology and physiology of a person. Examples of good emotions include taking caution rather than fear, wishing for something rather than developing an intense craving, affection towards others, goodwill and joy. The virtues also contribute to the reshaping of a person's entire personality from an emotional standpoint.

- **Having Virtues Leads a Person to Lead the Highest Quality of Life**

According to the Stoics, the more virtuous a person is, the happier he is. Therefore, developing the four virtues is only a means to living a happy life. People living in the early times, similar to those living currently, conceived happiness objectively as the natural life for human beings and as a subjective feeling that depends on the events of the day, which is how people conceive happiness today. However, the Stoics believe that virtue is the only means to feeling good and that it is necessary and sufficient for achieving happiness.

This belief was different from an earlier understanding where happiness was considered an amalgamation of both virtue and material things like riches, health, possessions and the wellness of the family. A kindhearted wealthy person was taken to be one of the happiest people alive. However, although the Stoics recognized the value of material things, they believed that virtue adds a significantly different kind of value and happiness and that on its own, virtue could confer complete happiness.

The Stoic way of describing happiness has always been thought to be extreme and unrealistic. It is obvious that a life that has an abundance of both virtue and material things is better, and will feel happier in every sense, compared to a life founded on virtues alone. However, the Stoics defend their position by stating that by itself, virtue is a consistent and reliable basis for leading a satisfying life but on their own, material things are not sufficient to provide happiness.

Therefore, even when you combine virtue and material things, happiness will remain pegged on virtue. From that understanding, virtue is of a value different from that of external goods, which is the reason the Stoics refused to take the combination of virtue and riches as the key to living a happy life.

In conclusion, it is important to keep in mind the relevance that the Stoics gave to virtues. That they help grow expertise and knowledge of dealing with life from all spheres, and that the expertise redefines the whole personality. It is also true that the virtues become a target or set the boundaries for aspirations. Virtues also lead one of the happiest lives. Overall, the Stoics believed that consistent and reliable virtuous living is the key to happiness.

9

Daily Practices for Modern Life

The concepts, techniques, and strategies that Stoic philosophers came up with act as aids for personal development and self-help purposes. It requires self-discipline, for which Stoics are known for upholding. Persons pursuing this lifestyle can take on some daily practices to help them adopt the Stoic lifestyle.

Below is a simple regimen:

Early morning Regimen

Meditation: Meditating in the morning allows you to calm your brain and collect your thoughts before you prepare for the day. As you stay still, the attention at this time should purely be focused on the inside, into yourself and in a way that isolates you from others. To do this effectively, walk in silence in a serene and pleasant environment.

Realize your place in the universe: The view of the rising sun or the stars as the day breaks helps to put things into perspective, especially when you focus on the cosmos and the place you hold in it. Next, give thanks because you have woken up, have a privileged life, and breathe that others do not have.

Keep account of your virtues and vices: Pick a personal strength or philosophical precept you would like to cultivate and come up with ways to incorporate it into your schedule. Think of how you will deal with tough situations that may arise.

Carry out prospective meditation: During this time, take note of any potential challenges of the day ahead, and figure out what will do, what you will say and what you will do about what others do. Rehearse in your mind the principles you will require to deal with the challenges that will arise wisely, perhaps drawing back to the self-analysis you performed the previous night.

When planning these activities, it is important that you take into account even the seemingly trivial issues like a bathroom visit because if you imagine the things that could potentially go wrong or hinder your plans, you are likely to be at peace and in alignment with nature.

Remind yourself that you only have control over your thoughts and actions; all other things are beyond control.

Think about possible catastrophes like sudden illness, bereavement, poverty, and your death: Rehearse how you would handle yourself facing these calamities rational composure to overcome the attachment you have to the things mentioned above. Think about how uncertain the future is and the need to enjoy life here and now.

View from Above: This is an exercise designed to help you see how small you are in the world, and how minute things and issues really are. In other words, this exercise allows you to see the bigger picture. It is simple because you only use your imagination to try to relate yourself to the entire world.

Contemplate the ideal woman or man: From time to time, think about the ideal man or woman, and his qualities. For now, only focus on psychological ideals. Think about his ideal character and his inner qualities. What would be his philosophical attitude when faced with the circumstances that you are faced with? This exercise is intended to be a catalyst that will make you a better human being.

The Day Regimen

The activities of the day are separate from those of the morning. Here are a number of things to keep you busy in your day:

Practice the mindfulness of the ruling faculty: This exercise is meant to help you identify with your true nature as a rational person and to help you learn how to prize wisdom and other virtues as the primary good in life. Use this thought process to assess your actions, character, and judgments in any given situation.

Practice indifference and acceptance: Learn to view the things of the external environment with some indifference. Remind yourself that everything can be beneficial if you wish it to be because you have the power to derive benefits from your experiences. Some say that what does not kill you will make you stronger. Seek to be strong in the face of disappointment and adversity.

Determine the profit you get by viewing life as a chain of transactions where you sell your judgments and your actions, and in return get experiences: Virtue is always counted as a profit and as a reward although it leads to other profits as well like friendships. Accepting that you will experience some losses also is important for your sanity. However, if the price you pay is that you end up enslaved to things and other people, quickly renounce them and profit by obtaining your freedom back because upon that, you will get a higher value.

Cultivate philanthropy: Philanthropy is simply having the desire to see others through good things, those that promote their welfare. Having and giving money is not the only way to be philanthropic; it only requires you to have the right attitude toward other people. To cultivate philanthropy, try bringing more people to your nearer circle. Think of your family as of yourself and other people as family.

Cognitive distancing: Develop the ability to separate events and their causes. For example, when you are upset, remind yourself that you judged that upset you and not external events or the actions of others. Primarily, do not allow yourself to be carried away by impression. Instead, take time before you respond to a situation and 0only do so when you have regained some sense of self-control and composure.

Use empathy to understand others: If someone is unkind to you, or opposes you or insults you, remind yourself that he is only doing what appears to be right to him and he didn't know better. Set aside your value judgment and only dwell on a bare description of his behavior because he can only interpret what he did as bad based on his intentions and value judgments.

Affinity and cosmic consciousness: Think of yourself as a part of the entire universe by taking in space and time as one thing, with you inside it. Imagine that this interconnection depends on each constituent, including you.

Invoke the reserve clause: Rather than going by the feelings you have, both for and against, use your judgment to guide through voluntary actions either away or towards things, but only do this without straining, adding the 'God willing' or 'fate permitting' clause to every intention that depends on external factors to succeed.

Self-Retreat: People believe that a change of scenery will offer them peace of mind, but this is deeply unphilosophical because freedom and peace of mind come from within. The easier way to achieve peace and freedom is to retreat inside your mind regularly. The mind is the most freeing place, and all that you need is ten minutes every day, shut the world outside and look deep inside your mind.

Take yourself through physical exercises to train self-control: The ability to give up unnecessary desires and to endure hardship helps you withdraw your focus from things that are beyond control to your voluntary actions and judgments. The physical exercise is not meant to attack your body but to build your psychological endurance.

The Evening Regimen

In your mind, review the happenings of the day at least three times, from start to finish, and even on previous days if need be. If something is amiss, try to figure out the mistakes you might have made and condemned those actions rationally and moderately. Evaluate the wisdom or strength you showed, and sincerely praise yourself for doing well. Figure out what you could have done better so that you do it right the next time it recurs.

Keep a philosophical journal: In this journal, you need to analyze and not just list what happened during the day. This journal can be a tool for self-discovery. It also shows the progress you are making over time. By constantly reflecting on what you write, you can improve your future and current life. Plan the events of the future based on an ethical framework and later look back on what has happened, using it to determine areas that need improvement.

The stripping exercise: This exercise is based on the assumption that every situation as layers like that of an onion. Each layer is a representative of what you have brought into the situation, and it is only by reaching the core issues that we can get to act according to the proper ethical frameworks. Do not consider your gains or your reputation in this exercise and instead think of the value the solution could bring to everyone and the qualities the situation requires. If you have these qualities, then that is a good thing, and if not, take this as the chance to acquire them.

Negative Visualization: Many times, we get used to having things and even begin to take them for granted. However, negative visualization reminds us how lucky we are based on a very simple premise of imagining that something bad has happened. You could have lost all your possessions, a family member, your sight and many other catastrophes. This pessimism is meant to help you realize that you still have it good and that things could have gone worse, enabling you to see the positive side of things as at now.

Relax and sleep: With the day and its events behind you, develop an attitude of satisfaction and contentment, pleased with how your life has turned out so far. Now, silence your mind, stretch out your body so that your sleep is as tranquil, and composed as possible.

The steps above, when practiced as a daily drill, are sure to produce the happiest, most contented and good-natured person out of you. You will be able to live the Stoic good life and get the opportunity to seek the welfare of others besides your own.

Conclusion

Thank you for making it through to the end of *Stoicism: A Guide in Modern Society*, let's hope it was informative and able to provide you with all of the tools you need to achieve your goals whatever they may be. Certainly, you were perplexed by the applicability of an old philosophy and model to life today. Many philosophies and ideals are quickly declared redundant by modernization through increased civilization and technological improvements, but not Stoicism.

Beginning from the third century, the Stoic way of life has been utilized and its foundations or ideologies have proven unshakeable. Stoicism is a well-founded theory with subjects, disciplines, virtues, principles, and applications. Its primary role is to encourage people to live happy lives by only caring about what is in their control, and letting nature take its course on issues that are beyond control. You certainly took note of the fact that Stoicism encourages its followers to take the path of least resistance, and instead, to take life as it comes. Of course, this is not meant to encourage complacency, but it encourages people to avoid losing battles and instead, focus on what is of most importance and benefit in life.

The next step is to get your feet wet and to begin to apply and take up the principles, virtues, disciplines and the lessons you have learned. It is of no use reading and understanding without testing them for yourself to know whether they work. You may find that you will lead a happier life, focused on the important things of life, and eventually be able to achieve much more than anticipated.

Begin the journey to true happiness today, and take up the daily practices for yourself. Teach others to do the same, and become part of the movement that teaches people how to be happy without letting life pass you by.

Finally, if you found this book useful in any way, a review on Amazon is always appreciated!

54542199R00074

Made in the USA
Columbia, SC
01 April 2019